'Michelle Zauner has picked up a legion of fans this year in a deeply personal memoir about growing up as an Asian American woman in the US, the impact of losing her mother and how her heritage, food and family has shaped who she is today.'

*Stylist*, 'The best books to gift for Christmas 2021'

'"Stop crying! Save your tears for when your mother dies," Michelle Zauner's mother drilled into her. *Crying in H Mart* is the result, a book about grief, Korean–US identity and Zauner's complex memories of her dead parent. Korean food linked them, music parted them: the author fronts indie band Japanese Breakfast.'

*Financial Times*, 'Books of the Year 2021: Pop'

'In the musician's gutting account of coming to terms with her mother's death and coming into her own as a Korean American, food is her lifeline.'

*New York Times*, 'Notable Books, 2021'

'Devastating . . . As Zauner unpacks the alienating specifics of growing up in Oregon as a biracial Korean American immigrant, and her rise in indie rock, her stories teem with sumptuous descriptions of Korean dishes that envelop the reader in a saliva-inducing experience . . . Underneath the swirl of glossy noodles and crispy snacks, *Crying in H Mart* is the tale of an artist resisting the voices that told her she couldn't make it, and finding self-actualization through the lifelong project of processing grief.'

*Pitchfork*, 'Best Music Books of 2021'

'Grief, anxiety and the many flavours of instant noodles suffuse this story of loss, growth and mother–daughter love . . . *Crying in H Mart* takes the measure of the complex bond and the impassable, yet tender, interval between mother and daughter . . . Zauner performs the work of creative memory that recovers and transmutes the past into something liveable, with verve and honesty . . . A story of great loss and growth . . . It seems that in her art, she has found the tricky yet transformative key to her inheritance.'

*Guardian*

'Zauner writes with piercing emotional clarity . . . [and] remarkable, richly rendered detail . . . The result is a portrait of a mother–daughter relationship which is both tender and bracing in its candour.'

*Independent*

'Zauner's striking, food-focused memoir . . . leaves you hungry and heartbroken.'

*i-D*

'Like all good food writing, Zauner's debut book comes from the perspective of being open and honest about life's ups and downs, making savouring the moment and the flavours within all the more joyous and cathartic to experience. *Crying in H Mart* is as affecting as it is appetising.'

*Scotsman*

'This multifaceted and astute memoir that delves deep into the complicated relationship she had with her mother, who died from cancer when Zauner was twenty-five. *Crying in H Mart* is at once a testament to a lost loved one, a charting of the ravages of terminal illness and a celebration of a mixed-race heritage that helps one young woman manage her grief.'

*Irish Times*

'Highly evocative (smells seem to steam off the page), a vivid combination of reflective essay and memoir – but essentially a homage to her mother. What emerges, however, is the complexity of their relationship and the ambivalence of her feelings – her mother a mixture of tough love, hard task-master and devoted parent to her only daughter, who was always seeking ways to get her approval. Food, death, love, marriage, family, identity and art are just some of the preoccupations in this often moving self-portrait.'

*Sydney Morning Herald*

'Zauner brings dish after dish to life on the page in a rich broth of delectable details, cultural context and the personal history often packed into every bite. Michelle Zauner has accomplished the unthinkable: a book that caters to all appetites.'

*San Francisco Chronicle*

'*Crying in H Mart* powerfully maps a complicated mother–daughter relationship . . . Zauner writes about her mother's death [with] clear-eyed frankness . . . Zauner plumbs the connections between food and identity . . . Her food descriptions transport us to the table alongside her. What *Crying in H Mart* reveals is that in losing her mother and cooking to bring her back to life, Zauner became herself.'

*NPR*

'*Crying in H Mart* is filled with rich, reverential descriptions of food. This book will make you long for home cooking and contemplate the ways you construct your own identity – whether that's tied to your family, heritage, or career.'
*Vulture*

'*Crying in H Mart* [has become] *the* must-read memoir for very good reason: poignant, blisteringly honest, and generously vulnerable, Zauner's retelling of her family lore and the ways she pulled herself out of the brink of despair is impossible to put down.'
*Entertainment Weekly*

'Heartwrenching.'
MTV.com

'A heartbreakingly beautiful memoir.'
*Philadelphia Inquirer*

'A warm and wholehearted work of literature, an honest and detailed account of grief over time, studded with moments of hope, humor, beauty, and clear-eyed observation. It is not to be missed.'
*Seattle Times*

'*Crying in H Mart* – which chronicles Zauner's struggle to retain her Korean identity in the wake of her mother's death – is sure to establish her as a singular literary talent . . . Zauner's frankness around death feels like an unexpected yet deeply necessary gift.'
*Vogue US*, 'The Best Books to Read in 2021'

'Zauner's . . . memoir, about the death of her mother, her own life, and the centrality of food, *Crying in H Mart* is palpable in its grief and its tenderness, reminding us what we all stand to lose.'
*Vulture*, 'Most Anticipated Books of the Year'

'A candid, moving tribute to her mother, to her identity, and to our collective desire for connection in this often alienating world . . . Zauner's writing is powerful in its straight-forwardness, though some turns of phrases are as beautiful as any song lyric . . . but it is her ability to convey how her mother's simple offering of a rice snack was actually an act of the truest love that leaves the most indelible impression.'
Refinery29

'A beautiful, honest and stylish account of grief, food and heritage. The way Zauner writes about food and how it acts as a bridge between her and her mother, her culture, her sense of self, is brilliantly written.'
Nikesh Shukla, author of *Brown Baby*

'I read *Crying in H Mart* with my heart in my throat. In this beautifully written memoir, Michelle Zauner has created a gripping, sensuous portrait of an indelible mother–daughter bond that hits all the notes: love, friction, loyalty, grief. All mothers and daughters will recognize themselves – and each other – in these pages.'

Dani Shapiro, author of *Inheritance*

'*Crying in H Mart* is a wonder: A beautiful, deeply moving coming-of-age story about mothers and daughters, love and grief, food and identity. It blew me away, even as it broke my heart.'

Adrienne Brodeur, author of *Wild Game*

'*Crying in H Mart* stunned me – with its truthfulness and the force of its yearning. Beautiful, intimate, powerful, it is an unforgettable portrayal of grief and the bond between mother and daughter.'

Catherine Cho, author of *Inferno*

# Crying in H Mart

Michelle Zauner is best known as a singer and guitarist who creates dreamy, shoegaze-inspired indie pop under the name Japanese Breakfast. She has won acclaim from major music outlets around the world for releases like *Psychopomp* and *Soft Sounds from Another Planet*.

# Crying in H Mart

· A Memoir ·

MICHELLE ZAUNER

PICADOR

First published 2021 by Alfred A. Knopf
a division of Penguin Random House LLC, New York

First published in the UK in paperback 2021 by Picador

This edition first published 2022 by Picador
an imprint of Pan Macmillan
The Smithson, 6 Briset Street, London ECIM 5NR
*EU representative:* Macmillan Publishers Ireland Ltd, 1st Floor,
The Liffey Trust Centre, 117–126 Sheriff Street Upper,
Dublin 1, DOI YC43
Associated companies throughout the world
www.panmacmillan.com

ISBN 978-1-5290-3379-3

7 9 8

A CIP catalogue record for this book is available from the British Library.

Printed and bound by CPI Group (UK) Ltd, Croydon, CRO 4YY

Visit **www.picador.com** to read more about all our books
and to buy them. You will also find features, author interviews and
news of any author events, and you can sign up for e-newsletters
so that you're always first to hear about our new releases.

FOR

엄마

# CONTENTS

# CONTENTS

# Crying in H Mart

# Crying in H Mart

Ever since my mom died, I cry in H Mart.

H Mart is a supermarket chain that specializes in Asian food. The *H* stands for han ah reum, a Korean phrase that roughly translates to "one arm full of groceries." H Mart is where parachute kids flock to find the brand of instant noodles that reminds them of home. It's where Korean families buy rice cakes to make tteokguk, the beef and rice cake soup that brings in the New Year. It's the only place where you can find a giant vat of peeled garlic, because it's the only place that truly understands how much garlic you'll need for the kind of food your people eat. H Mart is freedom from the single-aisle "ethnic" section in regular grocery stores. They don't prop Goya beans next to bottles of sriracha here. Instead, you'll likely find me crying by the banchan refrigerators, remembering the taste of my mom's soy-sauce eggs and cold radish soup. Or in the freezer section, holding a stack of dumpling skins, thinking of all the hours that Mom and I spent at the kitchen table folding minced pork and chives into the thin dough. Sobbing near the dry goods, asking myself, Am I even Korean anymore if there's no one left to call and ask which brand of seaweed we used to buy?

Growing up in America with a Caucasian father and a Korean mother, I relied on my mom for access to our Korean heritage. While she never actually taught me how to cook (Korean people tend to disavow measurements and supply only cryptic instructions along the lines of "add sesame oil until it tastes like Mom's"), she did raise me with a distinctly Korean appetite. This meant a reverence for good food and a predisposition to emotional eating. We were particular about everything: kimchi had to be perfectly sour, samgyupsal perfectly crisped; stews had to be piping hot or they might as well have been inedible. The concept of prepping meals for the week was a ludicrous affront to our lifestyle. We chased our cravings daily. If we wanted the kimchi stew for three weeks straight, we relished it until a new craving emerged. We ate in accordance with the seasons and holidays.

When spring arrived and the weather turned, we'd bring our camp stove outdoors and fry up strips of fresh pork belly on the deck. On my birthday, we ate miyeokguk—a hearty seaweed soup full of nutrients that women are encouraged to eat postpartum and that Koreans traditionally eat on their birthdays to celebrate their mothers.

FOOD WAS HOW my mother expressed her love. No matter how critical or cruel she could seem—constantly pushing me to meet her intractable expectations—I could always feel her affection radiating from the lunches she packed and the meals she prepared for me just the way I liked them. I can hardly speak Korean, but in H Mart it feels like I'm fluent. I fondle the produce and say the words aloud—chamoe melon, danmuji. I fill my shopping cart with every snack that has glossy packaging decorated with a familiar cartoon. I think about the time Mom showed me how to fold the little plastic card that came inside bags of Jolly Pong, how to use it as a spoon to shovel caramel puffed rice into my mouth, and how it inevitably fell down my shirt and spread all over the car. I remember the snacks Mom told me she ate when she was a kid and how I tried to imagine her at my age. I wanted to like all the things she did, to embody her completely.

My grief comes in waves and is usually triggered by something arbitrary. I can tell you with a straight face what it was like watching my mom's hair fall out in the bathtub, or about the five weeks I spent sleeping in hospitals, but catch me at H Mart when some kid runs up double-fisting plastic sleeves of ppeongtwigi and I'll just lose it. Those little rice-cake Frisbees were my childhood, a happier time when Mom was there and we'd crunch away on the Styrofoam-like disks after school, splitting them like packing peanuts that dissolved like sugar on our tongues.

I'll cry when I see a Korean grandmother eating seafood noodles in the food court, discarding shrimp heads and mussel shells onto the lid of her daughter's tin rice bowl. Her gray hair frizzy, cheekbones protruding like the tops of two peaches, tattooed eyebrows rusting as the ink fades out. I'll wonder what my mom would have looked like in her seventies, if she'd have wound up with the same perm that every Korean grandma gets, as though it were a part of our race's evolution. I'll imagine our arms linked, her small frame leaning against mine as we take the escalator up to the food court. The two of us in all black, "New York style," she'd say, her image of New York still rooted in the era of *Breakfast at Tiffany's*. She would carry the quilted-leather Chanel purse that she'd wanted her whole life, instead of the fake ones that she bought on the back streets of Itaewon. Her hands and face would be slightly sticky from QVC anti-aging creams. She'd wear some strange high-top sneaker wedges that I'd disagree with. "Michelle, in Korea, every celebrity wears this one." She'd pluck the lint off my coat and pick on me—how my shoulders slumped, how I needed new shoes, how I should really start using that argan-oil treatment she bought me—but we'd be together.

If I'm being honest, there's a lot of anger. I'm angry at this old Korean woman I don't know, that she gets to live and my mother does not, like somehow this stranger's survival is at all related to my loss. That someone my mother's age could still have a mother. Why is she here slurping up spicy jjamppong noodles and my mom isn't? Other people must feel this way. Life is unfair, and sometimes it helps to irrationally blame someone for it.

Sometimes my grief feels as though I've been left alone in a room with no doors. Every time I remember that my mother is dead, it feels like I'm colliding with a wall that won't give. There's no escape, just a hard surface that I keep ramming into over and over, a reminder of the immutable reality that I will never see her again.

H MARTS are usually situated on the outskirts of the city and serve as a secondary center for strip malls of Asian storefronts and restaurants that are always better than the ones found closer to town. We're talking Korean restaurants that pack the table so full of banchan side dishes that you're forced to play a never-ending game of horizontal Jenga with twelve tiny plates of stir-fried anchovies, stuffed cucumbers, and pickled everything. This isn't like the sad Asian fusion joint by your work, where they serve bell peppers in their bibimbap and give you the stink eye when you ask for another round of wilted bean sprouts. This is the real deal.

You'll know that you're headed the right way because there will be signs to mark your path. As you go farther into your pilgrimage, the lettering on the awnings slowly begins to turn into symbols that you may or may not be able to read. This is when my elementary-grade Korean skills are put to the test—how fast can I sound out the vowels in traffic? I spent more than six years going to Hangul Hakkyo every Friday, and this is all I have to show for it. I can read the signs for churches, for an optometrist's office, a bank. A couple more blocks in, and we're in the heart of it. Suddenly, it's another country. Everyone is Asian, a swarm of different dialects crisscross like invisible telephone wires, the only English words are HOT POT and LIQUORS, and they're all buried beneath an assortment of glyphs and graphemes, with an anime tiger or a hot dog dancing next to them.

Inside an H Mart complex, there will be some kind of food court, an appliance shop, and a pharmacy. Usually, there's a beauty counter where you can buy Korean makeup and skin-care products with snail mucin or caviar oil, or a face mask that vaguely boasts "placenta." (Whose placenta? Who knows?) There will usually be a pseudo-French bakery with weak coffee, bubble tea, and an array of glowing pastries that always look much better than they taste.

My local H Mart these days is in Elkins Park, a town northeast of Philadelphia. My routine is to drive in for lunch on the weekends, stock up on groceries for the week, and cook something for dinner with whatever fresh bounty inspires me. The H Mart in Elkins Park has two stories; the grocery is on the first floor and the food court is above it. Upstairs, there is an array of stalls serving different kinds of food. One is dedicated to sushi, one is strictly Chinese. Another is for traditional Korean jjigaes, bubbling soups served in traditional earthenware pots called ttukbaegis, which act as mini cauldrons to ensure that your soup is still bubbling a good ten minutes past arrival. There's a stall for Korean street food that serves up Korean ramen (basically just Shin Cup noodles with an egg cracked in); giant steamed dumplings full of pork and glass noodles housed in a thick, cakelike dough; and tteokbokki, chewy, bite-sized cylindrical rice cakes boiled in a stock with fish cakes, red pepper, and gochujang, a sweet-and-spicy paste that's one of the three mother sauces used in pretty much all Korean dishes. Last, there's my personal favorite: Korean-Chinese fusion, which serves tangsuyuk—a glossy, sweet-and-sour orange pork—seafood noodle soup, fried rice, and black bean noodles.

The food court is the perfect place to people-watch while sucking down salty, fatty jjajangmyeon. I think about my family who lived in Korea, before most of them died, and how Korean-Chinese was always the first thing we'd eat when my mom and I arrived in Seoul after a fourteen-hour flight from America. Twenty minutes after my aunt would phone in our order, the apartment ringer would buzz "Für Elise" in MIDI, and up would come a helmeted man, fresh off his motorcycle, with a giant steel box. He'd slide open the metal door and deliver heaping bowls of noodles and deep-fried battered pork with its rich sauce on the side. The plastic wrap on top would be concave and sweating. We'd peel it off and dribble black, chunky goodness all over the noodles and pour the shiny, sticky, translucent orange sauce over the pork. We'd sit cross-legged on the cool marble floor, slurping and reaching over one another. My aunts and mom and grandmother would jabber on in Korean, and I would eat and listen, unable to comprehend, bothering my mom every so often, asking her to translate.

I wonder how many people at H Mart miss their families. How many are thinking of them as they bring their trays back from the different stalls. If they're eating to feel connected, to celebrate these people through food. Which ones weren't able to fly back home this year, or for the past ten years? Which ones are like me, missing the people who are gone from their lives forever?

At one table is a group of young Chinese students, alone without family at schools in America. They have banded together to take the bus forty-five minutes outside the city, into the suburbs of a foreign country for soup dumplings. At another table, there are three generations of Korean women eating three different types of stew: daughter, mother, and grandmother dipping their spoons into one another's bowls, reaching over one another's trays, arms in one another's faces, pinching at their different banchan with chopsticks. None of them pay any heed or give a second thought to the concept of personal space.

There is a young white man and his family. They giggle together as they try to pronounce the menu. The son explains to his parents the different dishes they've ordered. Maybe he was stationed in Seoul for military service or taught English abroad. Maybe he's the only one in his family with a passport. Maybe this will be the moment his family decides it's time to travel and discover these things themselves.

There is an Asian guy blowing his girlfriend's mind, introducing her to a new world of flavors and textures. He shows her how to eat mul naengmyeon, a cold noodle soup that tastes better if you add vinegar and hot mustard first. He tells her how his parents came to this country, how he watched his mom make this dish at home. When she made it, she didn't add zucchini; she subbed radishes instead. An old man hobbles over to a neighboring table to order the chicken-and-ginseng porridge that he probably eats here every day. Bells go off for people to collect their orders. Behind the counters, women in visors work without stopping.

It's a beautiful, holy place. A cafeteria full of people from all over the world who have been displaced in a foreign country, each with a different history. Where did they come from and how far did they travel? Why are they all here? To find the galangal no American supermarket stocks to make the Indonesian curry that their father loves? To buy the rice cakes to celebrate Jesa and honor the anniversary of their loved one's passing? To satisfy a craving for tteokbokki on a rainy day, moved by a memory of some drunken, late-night snack under a pojangmacha tent in Myeong-dong?

We don't talk about it. There's never so much as a knowing look. We sit here in silence, eating our lunch. But I know we are all here for the same reason. We're all searching for a piece of home, or a piece of ourselves. We look for a taste of it in the food we order and the ingredients we buy. Then we separate. We bring the haul back to our dorm rooms or our suburban kitchens, and we re-create the dish that couldn't be made without our journey. What we're looking for isn't available at a Trader Joe's. H Mart is where your people gather under one odorous roof, full of faith that they'll find something they can't find anywhere else.

In the H Mart food court, I find myself again, searching for the first chapter of the story I want to tell about my mother. I am sitting next to a Korean mother and her son, who have unknowingly taken the table next to ol' waterworks. The kid dutifully gets their silverware from the counter and places it on paper napkins for both of them. He's eating fried rice and his mom has seolleongtang, ox-bone soup. He must be in his early twenties, but his mother is still instructing him on how to eat, just like my mom used to. "Dip the onion in the paste." "Don't add too much gochujang or it'll be too salty." "Why aren't you eating the mung beans?" Some days, the constant nagging would annoy me. Woman, let me eat in peace! But, most days, I knew it was the ultimate display of a Korean woman's tenderness, and I cherished that love. A love I'd do anything to have back.

The boy's mom places pieces of beef from her spoon onto his. He is quiet and looks tired and doesn't talk to her much. I want to tell him how much I miss my mother. How he should be kind to his mom, remember that life is fragile and she could be gone at any moment. Tell her to go to the doctor and make sure there isn't a small tumor growing inside her too.

Within five years, I lost both my aunt and my mother to cancer. So, when I go to H Mart, I'm not just on the hunt for cuttlefish and three bunches of scallions for a buck; I'm searching for memories. I'm collecting the evidence that the Korean half of my identity didn't die when they did. H Mart is the bridge that guides me away from the memories that haunt me, of chemo head and skeletal bodies and logging milligrams of hydrocodone. It reminds me of who they were before, beautiful and full of life, wiggling Chang Gu honey-cracker rings on all ten of their fingers, showing me how to suck a Korean grape from its skin and spit out the seeds.

# Save Your Tears

My mother died on October 18, 2014, a date I'm always forgetting. I don't know why exactly, if it's because I don't want to remember or if the actual date seems so unimportant in the grand scheme of what we endured. She was fifty-six years old. I was twenty-five, an age my mother had assured me for years would be special. It was the same age my mother had been when she met my father. The year they got married, the year she left her home country, her mother, and two sisters and embarked on a pivotal chapter of her adult life. The year she began the family that would come to define her. For me, it was the year things were supposed to fall into place. It was the year her life ended and mine fell apart.

Sometimes I feel guilty about misremembering when it happened. Every fall I have to scroll through the photos I've taken of her gravestone to reconfirm the date engraved, half obscured by the multicolored bouquets I've left these past five years, or I resort to googling the obituary I neglected to write so I can prepare to willfully feel something that never quite feels like the thing I'm supposed to be feeling.

My father is obsessed with dates. Some sort of internal clock whirs without fail around every impending birthday, death day, anniversary, and holiday. His psyche intuitively darkens the week before and soon enough he'll inundate me with Facebook messages about how unfair it all is and how I'll never know what it's like to lose your best friend. Then he'll go back to riding his motorcycle around Phuket, where he retired a year after she died, filling the void with warm beaches and street-vended seafood and young girls who can't spell the word *problem*.


WHAT I NEVER seem to forget is what my mother ate. She was a woman of many "usuals." Half a patty melt on rye with a side of steak fries to share at the Terrace Cafe after a day of shopping. An unsweetened iced tea with half a packet of Splenda, which she would insist she'd never use on anything else. Minestrone she'd order "steamy hot," not "steaming hot," with extra broth from the Olive Garden. On special occasions, half a dozen oysters on the half shell with champagne mignonette and "steamy hot" French onion soup from Jake's in Portland. She was maybe the only person in the world who'd request "steamy hot" fries from a McDonald's drive-through in earnest. Jjamppong, spicy seafood noodle soup with extra vegetables from Cafe Seoul, which she always called Seoul Cafe, transposing the syntax of her native tongue. She loved roasted chestnuts in the winter though they gave her horrible gas. She liked salted peanuts with light beer. She drank two glasses of chardonnay almost every day but would get sick if she had a third. She ate spicy pickled peppers with pizza. At Mexican restaurants she ordered finely chopped jalapeños on the side. She ordered dressings on the side. She hated cilantro, avocados, and bell peppers. She was allergic to celery. She rarely ate sweets, with the exception of the occasional pint of strawberry Häagen-Dazs, a bag of tangerine jelly beans, one or two See's chocolate truffles around Christmastime, and a blueberry cheesecake on her birthday. She rarely snacked or took breakfast. She had a salty hand.

I remember these things clearly because that was how my mother loved you, not through white lies and constant verbal affirmation, but in subtle observations of what brought you joy, pocketed away to make you feel comforted and cared for without even realizing it. She remembered if you liked your stews with extra broth, if you were sensitive to spice, if you hated tomatoes, if you didn't eat seafood, if you had a large appetite. She remembered which banchan side dish you emptied first so the next time you were over it'd be set with a heaping double portion, served alongside the various other preferences that made you, you.

IN 1983 my father flew to South Korea in response to an ad in *The Philadelphia Inquirer* that read simply "Opportunity Abroad." The opportunity turned out to be a training program in Seoul, selling used cars to the U.S. military. The company booked him a room at the Naija Hotel, a landmark in the Yongsan district, where my mother worked the front desk. She was, supposedly, the first Korean woman he ever met.

They dated for three months and when the training program ended, my father asked my mother to marry him. The two of them made their way through three countries during the mid-'80s, living in Misawa, Heidelberg, and Seoul again, where I was born. A year later, my father's older brother Ron offered him a job at his truck brokerage company. The position afforded stability and an end to my family's biannual intercontinental uprooting, and so we immigrated when I was just a year old.

We moved to Eugene, Oregon, a small college town in the Pacific Northwest. The city sits near the source of the Willamette River, which stretches 150 miles north, from the Calapooya Mountains outside of town to its mouth on the Columbia. Carving its way between mountains, the Cascade Range to the east and the Oregon Coast Range to the west, the river defines a fertile valley where tens of thousands of years ago a series of ice age floods surged southwest from Lake Missoula, traveling over eastern Washington and bringing with their floodwaters rich soil and volcanic rock that now shore up the layers of its earth, alluvial plains fit for a vast variety of agriculture.

The town itself is coated in green, hugging the banks of the river and spreading out up into the rugged hills and pine forests of central Oregon. The seasons are mild, drizzly, and gray for most of the year but give way to a lush, unspoiled summer. It rains incessantly and yet I never knew an Oregonian to carry an umbrella.

Eugenians are proud of the regional bounty and were passionate about incorporating local, seasonal, and organic ingredients well before it was back in vogue. Anglers are kept busy in fresh waters, fishing for wild chinook salmon in the spring and steelhead in the summer, and sweet Dungeness crab is abundant in the estuaries year-round. Local farmers gather every Saturday downtown to sell homegrown organic produce and honey, foraged mushrooms, and wild berries. The general demographic is of hippies who protest Whole Foods in favor of local co-ops, wear Birkenstocks, weave hair wraps to sell at outdoor markets, and make their own nut butter. They are men with birth names like Herb and River and women called Forest and Aurora.

When I was ten we moved seven miles outside the city, out past the Christmas-tree farms and the hiking trails of Spencer Butte Park to a house in the woods. It sat on nearly five acres of land, where flocks of wild turkeys roamed picking for insects in the grass and my dad could drive his riding mower in the nude if he wanted to, shielded by thousands of ponderosa pines, no neighbors for miles. Out back, there was a clearing where my mother grew rhododendrons and kept the lawn kempt. Beyond it the land gave way to sloping hills of stiff grass and red clay. There was a man-made pond filled with muddy water and soft silt, and salamanders and frogs to chase after, catch, and release. Blackberry bramble grew wild and in the early summer, during the burning season, my father would take to it with a large pair of gardening shears and clear new pathways between the trees to form a circuit he could round on his dirt bike. Once a month he'd ignite the burn piles he'd gathered, letting me squeeze the lighter fluid onto their bases, and we'd admire his handiwork as the six-foot bonfires went up in flames.

I loved our new home but I also came to resent it. There were no neighborhood children to play with, no convenience stores or parks within biking distance. I was stranded and lonely, an only child with no one to talk to or turn to but my mother.

Left with her in the woods, I was overwhelmed by her time and attention, a devotion that I learned could both be an auspicious privilege and have smothering consequences. My mother was a homemaker. Making a home had been her livelihood since I was born, and while she was vigilant and protective, she wasn't what you would call coddling. She was not what I'd refer to as a "Mommy-Mom," which was what I envied most of my friends for having. A Mommy-Mom is someone who takes an interest in everything her child has to say even when there is no actual way she gives a shit, who whisks you away to the doctor when you complain of the slightest ailment, who tells you "they're just jealous" if someone makes fun of you, or "you always look beautiful to me" even if you don't, or "I love this!" when you give them a piece of crap for Christmas.

But every time I got hurt, my mom would start screaming. Not *for* me, but *at* me. I couldn't understand it. When my friends got hurt, their mothers scooped them up and told them it was going to be okay, or they went straight to the doctor. White people were always going to the doctor. But when I got hurt, my mom was livid, as if I had maliciously damaged her property.

Once, when I was climbing a tree in the front yard, the notch I used to hoist myself up gave out from under my foot. I slid two feet, dragging the skin of my bare stomach on the coarse bark as I tried to regain my footing, falling six feet onto my ankle. Crying, ankle twisted, shirt ripped, my stomach scraped and bloody on either side, I was not scooped into my mother's arms and taken to a medical professional. Instead, she descended upon me like a murder of crows.

"HOW MANY TIME MOMMY SAY STOP CLIMBING THAT TREE?!"

"Umma, I think I sprained my ankle!" I cried. "I think I have to go to the hospital!"

She hovered over my crumpled body screeching relentlessly as I writhed among the dead leaves. I could have sworn she threw a few kicks in.

"Mom, I'm bleeding! Please don't yell at me!"

"YOU WILL HAVE THIS SCAR FOREVER! AY-CHAM WHEN-IL-EEYA?!"

"I'm sorry, okay? I'm sorry!"

I apologized over and over again, sobbing dramatically. Big fat tears and insistent stuttering wails. I pulled myself toward the house with my elbows, gripping the dry leaves and cold dirt as I stiffly dragged my limp leg forward.

"Aigo! Dwaes-suh! That's enough!"

Hers was tougher than tough love. It was brutal, industrial-strength. A sinewy love that never gave way to an inch of weakness. It was a love that saw what was best for you ten steps ahead, and didn't care if it hurt like hell in the meantime. When I got hurt, she felt it so deeply, it was as though it were her own affliction. She was guilty only of caring too much. I realize this now, only in retrospect. No one in this world would ever love me as much as my mother, and she would never let me forget it.

"Stop crying! Save your tears for when your mother dies."

This was a common proverb in my household. In place of the English idioms my mother never learned, she coined a few of her own. "Mommy is the only one who will tell you the truth, because Mommy is the only one who ever truly love you." Some of the earliest memories I can recall are of my mother instructing me to always "save ten percent of yourself." What she meant was that, no matter how much you thought you loved someone, or thought they loved you, you never gave all of yourself. Save 10 percent, always, so there was something to fall back on. "Even from Daddy, I save," she would add.

MY MOTHER was always trying to shape me into the most perfect version of myself. When I was an infant, she pinched my nose because she was worried it was too flat. In my elementary years, she feared I was too short, so every morning before school she'd instruct me to hold the bars of my headboard and pull my legs in an effort to stretch them out. If I furrowed my brow or smiled too widely, she'd smooth my forehead with her fingers and instruct me to "stop making wrinkles." If I walked with a slouch, she'd push a palm between my shoulder blades and command, "Ukgae pee-goo!" "Shoulders straight!"

She was obsessed with appearances and spent hours watching QVC. She phoned in orders for cleansing conditioners, specialty toothpastes, and jars of caviar-oil scrubs, serums, moisturizers, toners, and anti-aging creams. She believed in QVC products with the zeal of a conspiracy theorist. If you questioned the legitimacy of a product, she'd erupt in its defense. My mom was wholeheartedly convinced that Supersmile toothpaste made our teeth five shades lighter and Dr. Denese's Beautiful Complexion three-piece skin-care kit shaved ten years off our faces. Her bathroom counter was an island full of glass pots and tinted jars she dipped, dabbed, rubbed, patted, and smoothed onto her face, religiously following a ten-step skin-care regimen that included a microcurrent wand for electrocuting wrinkles. Every night from the hall I could hear the clapping of her palms against her cheeks and the hum of pulsing electricity supposedly tightening her pores as she zipped and zapped, then applied layer after layer of cream.

Meanwhile, boxes of Proactiv toners piled up, shoved beneath the cabinet of my bathroom sink; bristles of a Clarisonic cleansing brush remained dry and mostly unused. I was too impatient to keep up with any kind of regimen my mother tried to impose, a source of contention that would escalate throughout my adolescence.

Her perfection was infuriating, her meticulousness a complete enigma. She could own a piece of clothing for ten years and it'd look like it'd never been worn. Never a speck of lint on a coat, a pill on a sweater, or a single scuff on a patent-leather shoe, whereas I was reprimanded constantly for destroying or abruptly losing even those belongings I most dearly cherished.

She applied the same fastidiousness to the household, which she kept immaculate. She vacuumed daily, and once a week she would have me run a duster along all the baseboards as she doused the hardwood floors in oil and smoothed them over with a washcloth. Living with my father and me must have felt like living with two oversized toddlers hell-bent on destroying her perfect world. Often my mother would erupt over some small disarray, and the two of us would look out at the same horizon and have no clue what was unclean or misplaced. If either of us spilled something on the carpet, my mother would react as though we had set it on fire. Instantaneously, she'd release a pained wail, rush to collect the QVC carpet cleaning sprays from under the sink, and push us aside for fear we would spread the stain. Then we would just hover over her in embarrassment, watching stupidly as she dabbed and sprayed at our errors.

The stakes got higher when my mother began amassing various collections of precious, delicate things. Each set had a special place in the home where it was neatly displayed and organized: Mary Engelbreit miniature painted teapots lining the bookshelves in the hallway; porcelain ballerinas on the entryway credenza, the one in third position missing two fingers, a daily reminder of the consequences of my oafishness; and blue-and-white Dutch houses on the kitchen windowsills filled with gin, two or three with corks sloppily dug into in some drunken stupor, to remind my father of his. Crystal Swarovski animals mounted the glass shelves of the living room armoire. Every birthday and Christmas, a new glistening swan, porcupine, or turtle found its place on the wall, adding to the prismatic light that projected across the living room in the early morning.

Her rules and expectations were exhausting, and yet if I retreated from her I was isolated and wholly responsible for entertaining myself. And so I spent my childhood divided between two impulses, engaging in the intrinsic tomboyish whims that led to her reprimands and clinging to my mother, desperate to please her.

Sometimes, when my parents would leave me at home with a sitter, I would line up her figurines on a serving tray and cautiously wash each animal in the sink with dish soap, then dry them off with paper towels. I would dust the shelves beneath and clean the glass with Windex, then try my best to reorganize them from memory, hoping my mother would return and reward me with affection.

I developed this compulsion to clean as a sort of protection ritual performed when I felt even the slightest bit abandoned, an eventuality that tormented my young imagination. I was haunted by nightmares and an intense paranoia of my parents dying. I imagined robbers breaking into our house and envisioned their murders in horrible detail. If they returned home late from a night out, I was convinced they'd gotten into a car accident. I was plagued by recurring dreams of my father, impatient with traffic, attempting to navigate a faulty shortcut that led their car off the edge of the Ferry Street Bridge, plummeting them into the Willamette River, where they would drown, unable to escape through the doors due to the water pressure.

Judging by her positive reaction to the weekly episode of the duster and the baseboards, I concluded that if my mother returned to an even cleaner home, she would promise never again to leave me behind. It was my sad attempt to try to win her over. Once, on a vacation in Las Vegas, my parents left me alone in the hotel room for a few hours so they could gamble at the casinos. I spent the entire time tidying the room, organizing my parents' luggage, and wiping down the surfaces with a hand towel. I couldn't wait for them to return and see what I had done. I sat on my rollaway cot and just beamed at the door, waiting to see their faces, oblivious to the fact that housekeeping would come the next morning. When they returned, insensible to the changes, I quickly moved across the room, dragging them along with me as I pointed out my good deeds one by one.

I WAITED DESPERATELY for other such opportunities to shine and in my search for favorable proving grounds discovered that our shared appreciation of Korean food served not only as a form of mother-daughter bonding but also offered a pure and abiding source of her approval. It was at Noryangjin Fish Market on a summer trip to Seoul that this notion truly blossomed. Noryangjin is a wholesale market where you can choose live fish and seafood from the tanks of different vendors and have them sent up to be prepared in a number of cooking styles at restaurants upstairs. My mother and I were with her two sisters, Nami and Eunmi, and they had picked out pounds of abalone, scallops, sea cucumber, amberjack, octopus, and king crab to eat raw and boiled in spicy soups.

Upstairs, our table filled immediately with banchan dotting around the butane burner for our stew. The first dish to arrive was sannakji—live long-armed octopus. A plate full of gray-and-white tentacles wriggled before me, freshly severed from their head, every suction cup still pulsing. My mom took hold of one, dredged it through some gochujang and vinegar, placed it between her lips, and chewed. She looked at me and smiled, seeing my mouth agape.

"Try it," she said.

In marked contrast to the other domains of parental authority, my mother was loose when it came to the rules regarding food. If I didn't like something, she never forced me to eat it, and if I ate only half my portion, she never made me finish the plate. She believed food should be enjoyed and that it was more of a waste to expand your stomach than to keep eating when you were full. Her only rule was that you had to try everything once.

Eager to please her and impress my aunts, I balanced the liveliest leg I could find between my chopsticks, dipped it into the sauce as my mother had, and slipped it into my mouth. It was briny, tart, and sweet with just a hint of spice from the sauce, and very, very chewy. I gnashed the tentacle between my teeth as many times as I could before swallowing, afraid it would suction itself to my tonsils on the way down.

"Good job, baby!"

"Aigo yeppeu!" my aunts exclaimed. That's our pretty girl!

My family lauded my bravery, I radiated with pride, and something about that moment set me on a path. I came to realize that while I struggled to be good, I could excel at being courageous. I began to delight in surprising adults with my refined palate and disgusting my inexperienced peers with what I would discover to be some of nature's greatest gifts. By the age of ten I had learned to break down a full lobster with my bare hands and a nutcracker. I devoured steak tartare, pâtés, sardines, snails baked in butter and smothered with roasted garlic. I tried raw sea cucumber, abalone, and oysters on the half shell. At night my mother would roast dried cuttlefish on a camp stove in the garage and serve it with a bowl of peanuts and a sauce of red pepper paste mixed with Japanese mayonnaise. My father would tear it into strips and we'd eat it watching television together until our jaws were sore, and I'd wash it all down with small sips from one of my mother's Coronas.

Neither one of my parents graduated from college. I was not raised in a household with many books or records. I was not exposed to fine art at a young age or taken to any museums or plays at established cultural institutions. My parents wouldn't have known the names of authors I should read or foreign directors I should watch. I was not given an old edition of *Catcher in the Rye* as a preteen, copies of Rolling Stones records on vinyl, or any kind of instructional material from the past that might help give me a leg up to cultural maturity. But my parents were worldly in their own ways. They had seen much of the world and had tasted what it had to offer. What they lacked in high culture, they made up for by spending their hard-earned money on the finest of delicacies. My childhood was rich with flavor—blood sausage, fish intestines, caviar. They loved good food, to make it, to seek it, to share it, and I was an honorary guest at their table.

# 3

# Double Lid

Every other summer, while my father stayed behind to work in Oregon, my mother and I would travel to Seoul and spend six weeks with her family.

I loved visiting Korea. I loved being in a big city and living in an apartment. I loved the humidity and the smell of the city, even when my mother told me it was just garbage and pollution. I loved walking through the park across from my grandmother's apartment building, the sound of thousands of maemi flying overhead, their chattering cicada wings coalescing with the traffic noise at night.

Seoul was the opposite of Eugene, where I was stranded in the woods seven miles from town and at my mother's mercy to reach it. Halmoni's apartment was in Gangnam, a bustling neighborhood on the south bank of the Han River. Just through the park there was a small complex with a stationery shop, a toy store, a bakery, and a supermarket I could walk to unaccompanied.

From an early age, I loved supermarkets. I loved investigating every brand and its shiny, captivating packaging. I loved fondling ingredients and envisioning their endless possibilities and combinations. I could spend hours examining the freezers full of creamy melon bars and sweet red-bean popsicles, wandering the aisles in search of the plastic pouches of banana milk I drank every morning with my cousin Seong Young.

When my mother and I stayed in Seoul, Halmoni's three-bedroom apartment was shared among six people. You couldn't walk five feet without bumping into someone. Seong Young slept by the kitchen in a small, closet-sized room just big enough to accommodate a tiny square television, his Sony PlayStation, and a small futon mattress that lay beneath a rack of clothing across from the Mariah Carey poster he had taped to his door.

Seong Young was Nami Emo's son and my only cousin on my mother's side. His parents divorced shortly after he was born and, while Nami worked, he was largely raised by our grandmother in a house full of women. He was seven years older than me, tall and sturdily built, but moved about with a dejected posture, shy and effeminate in spite of his size. As a teenager he was extremely self-conscious, consumed by the pressures of school and his impending conscription, the two years of military service every Korean man is required to complete. He suffered from bad acne and would strenuously attempt to manage it with a variety of topical cleansers and creams, going so far as to wash his face exclusively with bottled water.

I adored Seong Young and spent the majority of my summers following him everywhere. He was a sweet boy, endlessly patient as I clung to his legs and back, forcing him to carry me through the humid summer heat while sweat poured from his face and soaked through his shirt, gracious when I begged him to chase me up the twenty-three flights of stairs to Halmoni's apartment.

Nami Emo's room was on the other side of the kitchen, abutting the small balcony that overlooked the street. She had a large, jade-colored vanity, its surface strewn with a hundred different kinds of nail polish. At the beginning of each visit, she would invite me to choose a color and after my careful deliberation, paint my nails on top of newspaper. When she was done, she'd use a special freezing spray from an aerosol can that helped them dry faster. The liquid would foam over my cuticles, then disappear like dry ice sneezed onto my fingertips.

Nami Emo was also the greatest storybook reader in the world. Like my grandfather before her, she worked as a voice actress, doing voice-overs for documentaries and dubbing anime episodes, which Seong Young and I would watch over and over on VHS. At night, she'd read Korean Sailor Moon books to me and do all the voices. It didn't matter that she couldn't translate the chapters into English—her voice was elastic and could swing seamlessly from the cackle of an evil queen to the catchphrase of the resolute heroine, then quiver words of caution from a useless sidekick and resolve with a dashing prince's gallant coo.

When I was eight or so, Nami Emo started dating Mr. Kim, whom I'd call Emo Boo after they married. Emo Boo wore his hair in a wide, black pompadour with a white streak, like Pepé Le Pew. He was a Chinese medicine doctor and ran his own clinic, drying, blending, and extracting natural ingredients to create herbal remedies. For my mother, Emo Boo's presence was a newfound weapon in her long-standing campaign to realize my ideal form. Every morning he would come to the apartment and brew a special herbal tea to help me grow and while we waited for it to steep, he'd insert acupuncture needles into my head to help stimulate my brain activity so I'd perform better at school.

The tea was dark green and smelled like black licorice mixed with tiger balm. It tasted like fruit rinds soaked in murky lake water and was the most bitter thing I'd ever consumed. Every day

I'd dutifully hold my nose and try to get as much of the hot syrupy liquid down as I could before gagging. Years later, in my twenties, I would come to realize the flavor profile matched the service industry's favorite bitter Italian spirit—Fernet.

Eunmi Emo's bedroom was opposite Nami's. She was the youngest sister and the only one to have attended college. She graduated at the top of her class with a major in English and would assume the role of translator when my mother became fed up with it and wanted to relax into her native tongue. She was only a few years younger than my mother, but perhaps because she'd never married or even dated, she felt more like a playmate than a guardian. I spent most of my days with her and Seong Young, rooting through their CD collections and begging them to chaperone visits to stationery shops filled with whatever new Korean character was in vogue that year—the Pajama Sisters, Blue Bear, or MashiMaro, the perverted rabbit who wore a plunger on his head.

At night my mother and I slept on a futon mattress in the living room, facing away from the glass sliding doors. I hated sleeping alone and relished the opportunity to sleep so close to her without the need for an excuse. At three a.m. we tossed and turned, tortured by jet lag. Eventually, my mother would turn and whisper, "Let's go see what's in Halmoni's refrigerator." At home, I was scolded if I got caught poking around the pantry past eight, but in Seoul, my mom was like a kid again, leading the campaign. Standing at the counter, we'd open every Tupperware container full of homemade banchan, and snack together in the blue dark of the humid kitchen. Sweet braised black soybeans, crisp yellow sprouts with scallion and sesame oil, and tart, juicy cucumber kimchi were shoveled into our mouths behind spoonfuls of warm, lavender kong bap straight from the open rice cooker. We'd giggle and shush each other as we ate ganjang gejang with our fingers, sucking salty, rich, custardy raw crab from its shell, prodding the meat from its crevices with our tongues, licking our soy sauce–stained fingers. Between chews of a wilted perilla leaf, my mother would say, "This is how I know you're a true Korean."

Most evenings my mother would linger in Halmoni's room. Every so often I'd observe them from the doorway as my mother lay beside her on a granite mattress on the floor, quietly watching Korean game shows as Halmoni chain-smoked cigarettes or peeled Asian pears with a large knife pulled toward her, all in one continuous strip. Halmoni would take bites from the core so none of the fruit would go to waste, while my mom ate from the perfectly cut slivers, just as I did when she cut fruit for me at home. It never occurred to me that she was trying to make up for all the years she'd spent away in America. It was difficult to even register that this woman was my mother's mother, let alone that their relationship would be a model for the bond between my mother and me for the rest of my life.

I was afraid of my grandmother. She spoke harshly and loudly and knew maybe fifteen words in English, so it always seemed like she was angry. She never smiled in pictures and her laugh was like a cackle that ended in loud hacking and coughing. She was as hunched over as an umbrella handle and always wore plaid pajama pants and shirts with glittering, rough fabrics. But I was chiefly afraid of one particular weapon she proudly brandished— the ddongchim. Ddongchim literally means *poop needle*. It involves clasping your hands in the shape of a gun, index fingers pressed together to create a needle used to penetrate an unsuspecting anus. As horrifying as it sounds, it's a common cultural thing, something akin to a Korean wedgie and not some unique form of sexual assault. Nevertheless, it scared the shit out of me. Whenever she was near, I constantly hid behind my mother or Seong Young, or scooted by her furtively with my butt pressed against the wall, anxiously expecting my halmoni to prod her index fingers through my pants, cackling and then hacking at my surprise and terror.

Halmoni loved to smoke, drink, and gamble, and especially loved partaking in all three around a deck of hwatu. Hwatu are small hard plastic cards roughly the size of a matchbook. The backs are a solid, brilliant red, and the faces are decorated with colorful illustrations of animals, flowers, and leaves. They are used to play a game called Godori, or Go-Stop, the goal of which is to match the cards in your hand with the cards laid out on the table. Roses match with roses, chrysanthemums with chrysanthemums, and each set corresponds to a point value. A set of ribbon cards is worth one point, a combination of three bird cards scores five. Five kwang, cards that are marked with a small red circle and the Chinese character for *bright,* are worth a whopping fifteen. Once you score three points, you can decide whether to "go" and try to collect more money, running the risk of another player overtaking your score, or "stop," finish the game and collect your earnings.

Most evenings, Halmoni would spread out her green felt blanket, grab her wallet, an ashtray, and a few bottles of soju and beer, and the women would play. Godori is not like other card games with their quiet moments of lead-up, analysis, sly reads, and coolheaded reveals. At least in my family, the games were loud and fast, my godmother, Jaemi, extending her arm a full three feet in the air before slapping her card down full force like a Pog slammer, the red plastic back whipping onto the face of its companion with an epic SMACK. The women would shout "PPEOK!" and "JOH TAH!" after every move, clanking together small silver towers of Korean won that grew and shrank over time.

While the women played hwatu, I played waitress. As a rule, Koreans eat when they drink, snacks collectively known as anju. I would empty bags of dried squid, peanuts, and crackers onto dishes from Halmoni's kitchen and serve them to my aunts and godmother. I'd bring them more beer and refill their glasses with soju or give them a Korean-style massage, which rather than a squeezing and rubbing of the shoulders is just a steady pounding on the back with the bottom of your clenched fists. When the game ended, the women would tip me from their winnings, and I'd run my greedy fingers over the imprint of Yi Sun-Sin's bearded face on a hundred-won coin or, if I was lucky, the soaring silver crane of a large five-hundred-won piece.

ONCE EVERY VISIT we would see my grandfather, always at the same Chinese restaurant, Choe Young Loo. He was a tall, lean man with a square jaw and gentle but masculine features. When he was younger, he wore his black hair slicked back in a neat pompadour, and looked svelte in colorful neckerchiefs and fitted designer jackets. He was a famous voice actor, known for his role as King Sejong on a popular radio broadcast, and when my mother was young their family was well-off. They were the first on their block to own a color television, and the neighborhood kids used to gather by the fence in their backyard and try to watch it through their living room window.

My grandfather had the looks to be a successful actor on screen but had trouble memorizing lines. As television rose in popularity, his career began to peter out. My mother used to tell me he had what Korean people call a "thin ear"—someone who is too easily swayed by the advice of others. A series of unsound investments saw him lose the family's savings by the time my mom had finished elementary school.

In an attempt to supplement their income, my grandmother sold homemade jewelry at outdoor markets. On weekdays she cooked large batches of yukgaejang, taking pounds of brisket, bracken root, radishes, garlic, and bean sprouts, and bubbling them into a spicy shredded-beef soup, which she would ladle into small plastic bags and sell to office workers on their lunch breaks.

Eventually, my grandfather left my grandmother for another woman and disowned the family. He only reached back out to his daughters years later to ask them for money. When Halmoni wasn't looking, my mother used to slip him an envelope after dinner and tell me to keep my mouth shut.

At the Chinese restaurant, Nami Emo would reserve a room with a big table and a gigantic glass lazy Susan on which turned small porcelain pitchers of vinegar and soy sauce with a marble button to ring for service. We'd order decadent jjajangmyeon noodles, dumpling after dumpling served in rich broth, tangsuyuk pork with mushrooms and peppers, and yusanseul, gelatinous sea cucumber with squid, shrimp, and zucchini. Halmoni would chain-smoke at one end of the table, silently watching as her husband caught up with the children he'd walked away from.

On the mezzanine, Seong Young would take me to see a six-foot-long fish tank that housed a baby alligator. It remained there year after year, blinking sleepily, until it grew so big it was unable to step forward even an inch, then disappeared altogether.

IN THE COURSE of one of these biannual visitations, at the age of twelve and nearing the peak of debilitating insecurity, I was confronted by a pleasant new discovery: I was pretty in Seoul. Everywhere we went strangers treated me like I was some kind of celebrity. Old ladies in shops would stop my mom to say, "Her face is so small!"

"Why do the ajummas keep saying that?" I asked my mother.

"Korean people like small faces," she said. "It looks better in pictures. That's why whenever we take a group photo people are always trying to push their head in the back. LA Kim always pushing my head forward."

LA Kim was one of my mother's oldest friends from high school. She was a big, jovial woman and she'd often make a joke out of craning her neck so the depth of field would make her face appear smaller.

"And Korean people like the double eyelid," my mother added, drawing a line between her eye and brow. I'd never noticed my mother did not have a crease, that the skin was smooth and flat. I scrambled to a mirror to find my reflection.

It was the first time I could remember being happy to have inherited something from my father, whose crooked teeth and too-long dip between nose and mouth I rued constantly. I wanted to grow up to look just like my mother, with perfect, smooth skin and three or four sporadic leg hairs I could just pluck out with a tweezer, but in that moment, what I wanted more than anything was to have the double lid.

"I have it! I have the double lid!"

"Many Korean women have surgery so they can have this one," she said. "Both Eunmi and Nami Emo had it. But don't tell them I told you."

In retrospect, I should have been able to hold up this information to my mother's obsession with beauty, to her affection for brand labels and all the hours she spent on skin care, and recognize in the source of her attitude a legitimate cultural difference rather than the caprice of her own superficial nagging. Like food, beauty was an integral part of her culture. Nowadays, South Korea has the highest rate of cosmetic surgery in the world, with an estimated one in three women in their twenties having undergone some type of procedure, and the seeds of that circumstance run deep in the language and mores of the country. Every time I ate well or bowed correctly to my elders, my relatives would say, "Aigo yep-peu." "Yeppeu," or *pretty,* was frequently employed as a synonym for *good* or *well-behaved,* and this fusion of moral and aesthetic approval was an early introduction to the value of beauty and the rewards it had in store.

I didn't have the tools then to question the beginnings of my complicated desire for whiteness. In Eugene, I was one of just a few mixed-race kids at my school and most people thought of me as Asian. I felt awkward and undesirable, and no one ever com-plimented my appearance. In Seoul, most Koreans assumed I was Caucasian, until my mother stood beside me and they could see the half of her fused to me, and I made sense. Suddenly, my "exotic" look was something to be celebrated.

Later in the week this glamorous realization would reach new heights of validation when Eunmi took us all to visit the Korean Folk Village, a living museum south of Seoul. Replicas of old-fashioned thatched-roof houses hugged its dirt roads, along which hundreds of hangari were strewn, red chiles beside them drying on woven mats, actors in traditional clothing here and there imper-sonating the peasants and royalty of the Joseon dynasty.

That day there happened to be a production of a K-drama period piece shooting. In between takes, the director noticed me and sent over his assistant. My mom nodded politely and took a business card, then erupted into laughter with her sisters.

"What did he say, Umma?"

"He asked me what your talents were."

Visions of life as a Korean idol flashed before me. My future six-pack gyrating in choreographed unison with four other K-idols in matching designer crop tops, the cartoon bubbles popping into the frame of my talk show appearances, throngs of teenagers con-gregating around my approaching limousine.

"What did you say?"

"I said you don't even speak Korean, and we live in America."

"I could learn Korean! Mom! If I stayed in Korea, I could be famous!"

"You could never be famous here, because you could never be anyone's doll," she said. My mother wrapped an arm around me and pulled my body toward her hip. A wedding party slowly passed in colorful traditional garb. The groom wore a maroon gwanbok and a stiff black hat of bamboo and horsehair fitted with thin silk flaps that hung from the sides. His bride was in blue and red, an elaborate silk topcoat over her hanbok with long sleeves that she kept connected in front of her like a muff. Her cheeks were painted with red circles.

"You don't even like it when Mommy tells you to wear a hat."

That was Mom, always seeing ten steps ahead. In an instant, she could envision a lifetime of loneliness and regimen, crews of men and women picking at my hair and face, choosing my clothes, instructing me on what to say, how to move, and what to eat. She knew what was best: to take the card and walk away.

Just like that, my hopes of living as a Korean idol were squashed, but for a short time I was pretty in Seoul, maybe even enough to have a shot at minor celebrity. If it wasn't for my mother, I might have wound up just like the pet alligator at the Chinese restaurant. Caged and gawked at in its luxurious confinement, unceremoniously disposed of as soon as it's too old to fit in the tank.

MY TIME with all these women and my cousin was like a perfect dream, but the reverie ended when Halmoni passed away. I was fourteen and in school when it happened, so I stayed behind when my mother flew to be with her mother at the hospital. Halmoni died the day my mother arrived, as if she had been waiting for her, waiting to be surrounded by all three of her daughters. In her bedroom she had wrapped the preparations for her funeral in a silk cloth. The outfit she wanted to be cremated in, the framed photograph she wanted displayed on her casket, money for the expenses.

When my mom returned from the funeral, she was devastated. She let out this distinctly Korean wail and kept calling out, "Umma, Umma," crumpled on the living room floor, her head heaving sobs into my father's lap as he sat on the couch and wept with her. I was afraid of my mother then, and I watched my parents shyly from afar, the same way I had watched my mother and her mother in Halmoni's room. I'd never seen my mother's emotions so unabashedly on display. Never seen her without control, like a child. I couldn't comprehend then the depth of her sorrow the way I do now. I was not yet on the other side, had not crossed over as she had into the realm of profound loss. I didn't think about the guilt she might have felt for all the years spent away from her mother, for leaving Korea behind. I didn't know the comforting words she probably longed for the way I long for them now. I didn't know then the type of effort it can take to simply move.

Instead I could only think of the last words my grandmother said to me before we returned home to America.

"You used to be such a little chickenshit," she said. "You never let me wipe your asshole." Then she let out a loud cackle, spanked me on the butt, and gave me a bony hug goodbye.

# 4

## New York Style

When I found out my mother was sick, I'd been out of college for four years and I was well aware I didn't have much to show for it. I had a degree in creative writing and film I wasn't really using. I worked three part-time jobs and played guitar and sang in a rock band called Little Big League that no one had ever heard of. I rented a room for three hundred dollars in North Philly, the same city where my father grew up and from which he eventually fled to Korea when he was around my age.

It was by sheer coincidence I'd wound up in Philadelphia. Like many a kid trapped in a small city, I felt bored and then suffocated. By the time I was in high school, the desire for independence trailing a convoy of insidious hormones had transformed me from a child who couldn't bear to sleep without her mother into a teenager who couldn't stand her touch. Every time she picked a ball of lint off my sweater or pressed her hand between my shoulder blades to keep me from slouching or rubbed her fingers on my forehead to ward off wrinkles, it felt like a hot iron puckering against my skin. Somehow, as if overnight, every simple suggestion made me feel like I was overheating, and my resentment and sensitivity grew and grew until they bubbled up and exploded and in an instant, uncontrollably, I'd rip my body away and scream, "Stop touching me!" "Can't you ever leave me alone?" "Maybe I want wrinkles. Maybe I want reminders that I've *lived* my life."

College presented itself as a promising opportunity to get as far away from my parents as possible, so I applied almost exclusively to schools on the East Coast. A college counselor thought a small liberal arts school, especially a women's college, would be a good fit for someone like me—captious and demanding of inordinate attention. We took a college trip and visited several schools. Bryn Mawr's stone architecture upright against the early signs of East Coast autumn seemed to measure up soundly to the ideal image of what we had always imagined a college experience should be.

It was somewhat of a miracle that I managed to get into college, having just barely graduated from high school. Senior year I had a nervous breakdown that resulted in a lot of truancy and therapy and medication, and my mother convinced all of it was a direct attempt to spite her, but somehow I managed to come out on the other side. Bryn Mawr was good for both of us, and I'd even graduated with honors, the first in my immediate family to obtain a college degree.

I decided to stick around Philadelphia because it was easy and cheap and because I was convinced Little Big League might some-day make it. But it had been four years now and the band had neither made it nor shown any real sign of spurning anonymity. A few months back I'd been fired from the Mexican fusion restaurant where I'd waitressed for a little over a year, the longest I'd managed to hold on to a job. I worked there with my boyfriend, Peter, whom I'd originally lured there in a long-game play to woo myself out of the friend zone, where I'd been exiled seemingly in perpetuity, but shortly after I finally won him over, I was fired and he was promoted. When I called my mom for a little sympathy, incredulous that the restaurant would fire such an industrious and charming worker as myself, she replied, "Well, Michelle, anyone can carry a tray."

Since then I had been working three mornings a week at a friend's comic shop in Old City, the other four days as a marketing assistant for a film distributor at an office in Rittenhouse Square, and weekends at a late-night karaoke and yakitori bar in Chinatown, all in an attempt to save up money for our band's two-week tour in August. The tour was planned in support of our second album, which we'd just finished recording, despite the fact that no one had really cared much about the first.

MY NEW HOME was a far cry from the one I'd grown up in, where everything was kept spotless and in its place, our furniture and decor carefully curated to my mother's specifications. Our living room had shelves made out of scrapped plywood and cinder blocks, which Ian, my drummer and roommate, had proudly salvaged from a trash heap. Our couch was a spare bench removed from the back of the fifteen-passenger van we used for touring.

My room was on the third floor. Across the hall was a small balcony that overlooked a baseball diamond where we could smoke cigarettes and watch Little League games in the summer. I enjoyed having a room on the top floor. The only real downside was that the ceiling in the closet was unfinished, exposing the beams and roofing, which never bothered me until a family of squirrels made its way through the roof and began copulating and nesting somewhere above. Sometimes at night, Peter and I would wake up to their scurrying and thudding around, which still wasn't so bad until one of them fell into the hollow space between the walls and, unable to escape, slowly died of starvation. Its carcass released a thick, rancid stench into my room, which also wasn't so horrible until in the unseen guts of the house, thousands of maggots spawned from the rot, breeding a plague of flies that confronted us one morning as I opened the bedroom door.

I had wound up doing exactly what my mother had warned me not to do. I was floundering in reality, living the life of an unsuccessful artist.

THAT MARCH I turned twenty-five, and by the second week of May I was starting to get antsy. I decided to head up to New York and meet with my friend Duncan, whom I'd known in college and who had since become an editor at *The Fader*. Privately, I was harboring a half hope that when the time came to finally give up on trying to be a musician, my interest in music might successfully parlay into a career in music journalism. As things stood, that time might be sooner than later. Deven, Little Big League's bass player, had recently started playing in another band that was gaining traction. They were set to perform on the Lower East Side that very weekend at a small club exclusively for press, which in itself seemed a sure-enough sign that Deven would not be in our band for much longer. They were, in Deven's words, on the path to becoming "Jimmy Fallon big." I wasn't quite ready to admit it, but I was going to New York that weekend, in part, to start laying the groundwork for something to fall back on.

The week before, my mother had mentioned she was having stomach problems. I knew she was scheduled to meet with a doctor that day, and I sent a few texts in the afternoon to follow up on her appointment. It was unlike her not to respond.

I boarded the Chinatown bus with a sinking feeling. My mother had mentioned a stomachache a couple months before that, in

February, but I didn't think much of it at the time. In fact, I'd made a joke out of it, asking in Korean if she had diarrhea: "Seolsa isseoyo?" It was a word I always remembered because it sounds a lot like *salsa* and, well, the similarity in texture made it easier to recall.

My mother rarely saw doctors, committed to the idea that ailments passed of their own accord. She felt Americans were overly cautious and overly medicated and had instilled this belief in me from a young age, so much so that when Peter got food poisoning from a bad can of tuna and his mother suggested I take him to urgent care, I actually had to stifle a laugh. In my household, there was nothing to do for food poisoning except throw it up. Food poisoning was a rite of passage. You couldn't expect to eat well without taking a few risks, and we suffered the consequences twice a year.

For my mother to see a doctor, something had to be fairly serious, but I never considered it could be something lethal. Eunmi had died of colon cancer just two years before. It seemed impossible that my mother could get cancer too, like lightning striking twice. Nevertheless, I began to suspect my parents were keeping a secret from me.

THE BUS ARRIVED in the early evening. Duncan suggested we meet at Cake Shop, a small bar on the Lower East Side that booked shows in the basement. I'd stuffed a hefty backpack full of clothes for the weekend and felt immediately frumpy and juvenile as I walked up Allen Street toward the bar.

Spring was giving way to summer and people getting off work were shedding their jackets, folding them over their forearms to carry. A familiar itch was creeping in. That aching toward something wild—when the days get longer and a walk through the city becomes entirely pleasant from morning to night, when you want to run drunk down an empty street in sneakers and fling all responsibility to the wayside. But for the first time it felt like an impulse I needed to turn away from. I knew there were no more summer vacations for me, no more idle days. I needed to accept that something, at some point soon, would have to change.

I got to the bar well before Duncan, who informed me he was running about twenty minutes late. I called my mom and got no answer. "What's going on???" I texted, beginning to feel neglected. I dropped my bag beneath a bar stool and leafed through the records by the front window.

I'd never been especially close friends with Duncan. He was two years older than me and a senior at Haverford when we met. Buses ran between our two campuses and students from either school could enroll in classes and clubs at either college. Duncan was one of five members of FUCs, a group that was in charge of booking the bands that came to play on campus. He'd advocated for me when I applied to join, and now I hoped he might look out for me again.

I felt my phone buzz. It was my mother, finally, so I grabbed my bag and slipped outside to take the call.

"Mom, what's going on?"

"Well, sweetie. We know you're in New York for the weekend," she said. "We wanted to wait until you were back in Philadelphia. When you're at home and with Peter."

Usually her voice trilled from the other end of the line, but now it sounded as if she spoke from a deadened room. I started to pace the block.

"If something's wrong I'd rather know now," I said. "It's not fair to keep me in the dark."

There was a long pause on the other end, one that indicated my mother had started the conversation with the intention of putting me off until I got home but was now beginning to reconsider.

"They found a tumor in my stomach," she said finally, the word falling like an anvil. "They say it's cancerous, but they don't know how bad it is yet. They have to run some more tests."

I stopped pacing, frozen and winded. Across the street a man was entering a barbershop. A group of friends sat at an outdoor table, laughing and ordering drinks. People were deciding on appetizers. Bumming cigarettes. Dropping off dry cleaning. Bagging dog droppings. Calling off engagements. The world moved on without pause on a pleasant, warm day in May while I stood silent and dumbfounded on the pavement and learned that my mother was now in grave danger of dying from an illness that had already killed someone I loved.

"Try not to worry too much," she said. "We will figure this out. Go and see your friend."

How? How how how? How does a woman in perfect health go to a doctor about an upset stomach and leave with a cancer diagnosis?

I could see Duncan turn the corner in the distance. He waved as I hung up. I swallowed the lump in my throat, slung my bag back over my shoulder, and smiled. I thought, Save your tears for when your mother dies.

HAPPY HOUR was buy one, get one free, so we ordered two bottles of Miller High Life with seconds on standby. We caught up on each other's postgraduate lives. He had just finished a cover story on Lana Del Rey and when I pressed him for details on the interview, he told me she chain-smoked through its entirety and recorded the whole thing on her iPhone to guard against misquotes, which endeared her to me.

On our second round I admitted I was entertaining the idea of moving to New York, fully aware that I was now speaking as a sort of character, mentally disavowing the information I'd learned only an hour before. I realized that any plans I might have had were now null and void, that I'd probably have to move back to Eugene to be there for my mother's treatment. I was delirious with secrecy. It was against my nature to withhold such monumental information, but it felt entirely inappropriate to bring it up to someone I knew only marginally, and I was afraid if I even said the words out loud I'd start crying.

Duncan was supportive of the move and encouraged me to reach out again when the time came. We said our goodbyes and I called Peter from the same stretch of sidewalk where I'd learned two hours prior that my mother had cancer.

PETER WAS THE FIRST PERSON I dated that my mother had ever liked. They met for the first time in September of the previous year. My parents were celebrating their thirtieth anniversary in Spain and arranged to stop in Philadelphia beforehand. It'd been three years since they'd visited me on the East Coast, this the first time since graduation. I was determined to impress them with my knowledge of the city and my self-sufficient, albeit flimsy version of young adulthood, and so I spent weeks researching and reserving tables at the best restaurants in the city and planned a day trip to Elkins Park to show my mother the Korean neighborhood.

Peter drove us all out to Jong Ga Jib, a restaurant that specializes in soondubu jjigae, a spicy soft-tofu stew. My mother lit up as she browsed the menu, excited by the variety of dishes the Korean restaurants in Eugene lacked, picking out things my father would enjoy. Peter was recovering from a cold, so she suggested he order samgyetang, a hearty soup made from a whole chicken stuffed with rice and ginseng. For the table she ordered haemul pajeon "basak basak," a tactic she always employed to try to get the edges as crispy as possible. Over soondubu jjigae and crunchy, thick slices of seafood pancake, I told my mother about a Korean spa I'd heard about in the neighborhood, similar to the ones we went to in Seoul.

"They even have the scrub," I said.

"Really? They even have scrub? Should we all go?" my mother asked with a laugh.

"That sounds fun," Peter said.

Jjimjilbangs are typically separated by gender, with a communal area for both sexes to socialize in the loose-fitted, matching pajamas provided on entry. Inside the bathhouse, full nudity is standard. If Peter came with us it would mean he and my father would have to be naked together a little less than twenty-four hours after they first met.

Peter ate his soup dutifully, thanking my mother for the recommendation, and partook joyfully in the banchan on our table—miyeok muchim, slick seaweed salad dressed with tart vinegar and garlic; sweet and spicy dried squid; gamja jorim, buttery, candied potatoes in sweet syrup—all dishes he'd discovered a love for since we'd started dating. One of my favorite things about Peter was the way he closed his eyes when he ate something he really liked. It was as if he believed cutting off one of his senses amplified the others. He was bold and never made me feel like what I was eating was weird or gross.

"He eats like a Korean!" my mother said.

When Peter excused himself to use the bathroom, my parents hunched in toward the center of the table.

"I bet you he chickens out of the bathhouse," my dad said.

"I bet you a hundred dollars he's going to do it," my mother countered.

The next day in the spa lobby when it was time to separate, Peter moved toward the men's locker room without flinching. My mother shot my father the smug grin of a winner and rubbed her fingers together, expecting him to pay up.

The bathhouse was smaller than the ones we usually went to in Seoul. There were three tubs of varying temperatures—cold, warm, and hot—and across from them a dozen showerheads where women rinsed off, seated on miniature plastic stools. On the far end were a sauna and a steam room. My mother and I showered, then slowly eased our way into the hottest tub, sitting side by side on the slick blue tile. In a corner, sectioned off, three ajummas in their undergarments diligently scrubbed their subjects. Inside it was warm and quiet, the only sounds the continuous gushing stream of water that jetted out from the ceiling into the cold tub and the occasional smack of a scrubbing hand against the bare back of an anonymous woman.

"Did you shave your boji tul?" she said.

I crossed my legs tightly, mortified. "I trimmed it," I said with a blush.

"Don't do that," she instructed. "It looks slutty."

"Okay," I said, slinking deeper into the water. I could feel her gazing unhappily at the tattoos I'd accumulated despite her vehement disapproval.

"I like Peter," my mother said. "He's New York style."

Anyone who has actually lived in New York would be loath to describe Peter as "New York style." Though he'd attended NYU, Peter lacked the bristly nature and fast-paced hustle a West Coaster usually associates with an East Coast personality. He was patient and gentle. He balanced me out in the way my mother did my father, who like me was always in a rush, quick to give up on any task at the first sign of failure and delegate it to someone else. What my mother meant was that she liked that Peter proved early on that he was a stand-up guy.

"I'LL COME UP," Peter said over the phone. "As soon as I get off, I'll be there."

It was Friday night and he had the late shift at the bar. The sun was setting, the sky getting pink. I started toward the subway and told him not to bother. He wouldn't get off until two and it wasn't worth coming up for the night when I was already planning on taking the bus back in the morning.

I took the M train to Bushwick, where I was crashing at my friend Greg's for the night. Greg played drums in a band called Lvl Up and lived in a warehouse known as David Blaine's The Steakhouse that hosted DIY shows. He had five roommates who all slept in tiny lofted bedrooms they'd built themselves out of drywall. They reminded me of the tree forts where the Lost Boys slept in *Peter Pan.* I lay on the couch in the living room and felt numb. I wondered what their mothers thought when they visited. The conditions musicians put themselves in for cheap rent and the freedom to pursue their unconventional passions.

I remembered how after our scrubs, my mother suggested we stock up on groceries at H Mart, so that she could marinate some short rib at my house and I could have a taste of home after she left. How I held my breath as she entered my dilapidated home, waiting for her to pick it apart in all its squalor or serve up some of the same acerbic wisdom she proffered when I'd gotten fired, but instead, she made her way to the kitchen without a word of critique, squeezing past the collection of bikes propped against the wall without faltering. She even generously ignored the gaping hole in the back wall, to which our landlord had taken a hammer in a resourceful effort to warm the frozen pipes, revealing in the process the utter lack of fluffy pink insulation.

She didn't comment on how nothing in our kitchen cabinets

matched, that our dishware was made up of thrift store finds and spare parts from my roommates' parents' houses. She found the things she'd gifted me over the years—the orange LocknLock storage containers, the Calphalon pans—then pushed up her sleeves and spread the meat she'd bought from H Mart out on a cutting board and began to tenderize it with a mallet. I kept waiting for her to say something under her breath. I knew she saw all the things I did and more, her sharp eye tearing apart the used furniture and undusted corners and the chipped, mismatched plates in the same way she used to tear apart my weight and complexion and posture.

She had spent my whole life trying to protect me from living this way, but now she just moved about the kitchen with a smile, chopping green onions, pouring 7Up and soy sauce into a mixing bowl, tasting it with her finger, seemingly unbothered by the cockroach traps that lined the counters and the smudged fingerprints on the fridge, intent only on leaving a taste of home behind.

My mother had either finally given up, conceding in her efforts to try to shape me into something I didn't want to be, or she had moved on to subtler tactics, realizing it was unlikely that I'd last another year in this mess before I discovered she'd been right all along. Or maybe the three thousand miles between us had made it so she was just happy to be with me. Or maybe she'd finally accepted that I'd forged my own path and found someone who loved me wholly, and believed at last that I would end up all right.

PETER DROVE UP to New York anyway. He closed the restaurant at two and got to Greg's by four in the morning. Still sticky from blood-orange margaritas, refritos caked onto his jeans, he squeezed next to me on the couch and lay still as I cried into his gray college T-shirt, finally able to release the billow of emotions

I'd suppressed all day, grateful he hadn't listened when I told him not to bother. He didn't tell me until much later that my parents had called him first. That he had known she was sick before me, that he had promised them that he would be there when I found out. That he would be there through it all.

# 5

# Where's the Wine?

"Why won't you include me?" I whined into my cell phone as if I were tattling on an older child for neglecting me. As if I hadn't been invited to a birthday party.

"You have to live your life," my mother said. "You're twenty-five. It's an important year. Your dad and I can handle this together."

More news had come and none of it was good. Dr. Lee, an oncologist in Eugene, had diagnosed her with stage IV pancreatic cancer. There was a 3 percent chance of survival without surgery. With surgery, it would take months to recover, and even then, there was only a 20 percent chance of emerging cancer-free. My father was fighting for an appointment at MD Anderson in Houston for a second opinion. Over the phone my mom pronounced it "pancry-arty" cancer and "Andy Anderson," which led me to believe our only hope lay in the hands of some kind of *Toy Story* character.

"I *want* to be there," I insisted.

"Mom's afraid you two will fight if you come," my father admitted later. "She knows she has to put all her focus into getting better."

I assumed the seven years I'd lived away from home had healed the wounds between us, that the strain built up in my teenage years had been forgotten. My mother had found ample space in the three thousand miles between Eugene and Philadelphia to relax her authority, and for my part, free to explore my creative impulses without constant critique, I came to appreciate all the labors she performed, their ends made apparent only in her absence. Now we were closer than ever, but my father's admission revealed there were memories of which my mother could not let go.

FROM DAY ONE, I'm told, nothing about me was easy. By the time I was three, Nami Emo had dubbed me the "Famous Bad Girl." Running into things headfirst was my specialty. Wooden swings, door frames, chair legs, metal bleachers on the Fourth of July. I still have a dent in the center of my skull from the first time I ran headfirst into the corner of our glass-top kitchen table. If there was a kid at the party who was crying, it was guaranteed to be me.

For many years, I suspected my parents might have been exaggerating or that they were ill prepared for the realities of a child's temperament, but I have slowly come to accept, based on the unanimous recollection of multiple relatives, that I was a pretty rotten kid.

But the worst was yet to come, the tense years to which I knew my father was referring. By the second semester of eleventh grade, what could have passed up to that point for simple teenage angst had begun to escalate into a deeper depression. I had trouble sleeping and was tired all the time; I found it hard to muster the will to do much of anything. My grades had started falling and my mother and I were constantly at odds.

"You get it from my side, unfortunately," my father told me one morning over breakfast. "Bet you can't sleep either."

He was sitting at the kitchen table, slurping a bowl of cereal and reading the newspaper. I was sixteen and recovering from another blowout with my mother.

"Too much going on here," he said. He tapped on his temple without looking up and turned to the sports section.

My father was a recovered addict and had endured an adolescence far more troubled than my own. When he was nineteen, residing semi-permanently under the boardwalk in Asbury Park, he was caught selling methamphetamine to a police officer. He spent six weeks in jail before moving to a rehabilitation center in Camden County, where he became a guinea pig for a new psychotherapy treatment. He was made to wear a sign around his neck that read I'M A PEOPLE PLEASER and engaged in exercises in futility that would supposedly stimulate moral fiber. Every Saturday he dug a hole in the yard behind the institution, and every Sunday they made him fill it back up again. Any trouble I might be in seemed minor by comparison.

He attempted to console my mother, convince her it was a normal phase, something most teenagers ache in and out of, but she refused to accept it. I had always done well in school, and this shift coincided all too conveniently with the time to start applying to colleges. She saw my malaise as a luxury they'd paid for. My parents had given me too much and now I was full of self-pity.

She doubled down, morphing into a towering obelisk that shadowed my every move. She needled me over my weight, the width of my eyeliner, the state of my breakouts, and my lack of commitment to the toners and exfoliants she'd ordered for me from QVC. Everything I wore was an argument. I wasn't allowed to shut my bedroom door. After school, when my friends would head to one another's houses for weekday sleepovers, I was whisked away to extracurriculars, then stuck in the woods, left to grumble alone in my room with the door left open.

ONCE A WEEK I was allowed to sleep over at my friend Nicole's apartment, my sole respite from my mother's overbearing supervision. Nicole's relationship with her mom was the complete opposite of mine. Colette gave Nicole freedom to make her own decisions, and they actually seemed to enjoy spending time together.

Their two-bedroom apartment was painted in bright, bold colors and was full of cool vintage furniture and clothing from thrift shops. Longboards from Colette's teen years in California were stacked by the front door, and souvenirs from a year abroad when she taught English in Chile lined the windowsills. A porch swing hung from the ceiling in the living room; plastic craft-store flowers weaved through the chain links that suspended it.

I admired the way they seemed more like friends than mother and daughter, envied their thrifting trips to Portland. How idyllic it seemed when I'd watch them bake together in their apartment, pressing pizzelles out of homemade batter with the heavy metal iron they'd inherited from Colette's Italian grandmother, tracing dozens of intricate patterns into delicate, edible doilies, dreaming of the café Colette someday wished to open, a place where they could sell their baked goods and decorate the interior just like the home I found so creative and charming.

Observing Colette made me question my mother's dreams. Her lack of purpose seemed more and more an oddity, suspect, even anti-feminist. That my care played such a principal role in her life was a vocation I naively condemned, rebuffing the intensive, invisible labor as the errand work of a housewife who'd neglected to develop a passion or a practical skill set. It wasn't until years later, after I left for college, that I began to understand what it meant to make a home and just how much I had taken mine for granted.

But as a teenager newly obsessed with my own search for a calling, I found it impossible to imagine a meaningful life without a career or at least a supplemental passion, a hobby. Why did her interests and ambitions never seem to bubble up to the surface? Could she truly be content as only a homemaker? I began to interrogate and analyze her skill set. I suggested possible outlets—courses at the university in interior design or fashion; maybe she could start a restaurant.

"Too much work! You know Gary's mom start her Thai restaurant—now she always running around! Never have time for anything."

"When I'm at school, what do you do all day?"

"I do a lot, okay! You just don't understand because you spoiled. When you move out of house you see everything Mommy do for you."

I could tell my mother was jealous of Colette—not because of her whimsical ambitions, but because of how I idolized her desultory aims—and the more I rotted into a cruel teenager, the more I flaunted my relationship with Colette as a way of taking advantage of my mother's emotions. I felt it was payback for how frequently she took advantage of mine.

INTO THE VACUUM of my disinterest, music rushed to fill the void. It cracked a fissure, splintered a vein through the already precarious and widening rift between my mother and me; it would become a chasm that threatened to swallow us whole.

Nothing was as vital as music, the only comfort for my existential dread. I spent my days downloading songs one at a time off LimeWire and getting into heated discussions on AIM about whether the Foo Fighters' acoustic version of "Everlong" was better than the original. I pocketed my allowance and lunch money to spend exclusively on CDs from House of Records, analyzing lyrics in the liner notes, obsessing over interviews with the champions of Pacific Northwest indie rock, memorizing the rosters of labels like K Records and Kill Rock Stars, and plotting which concerts I'd attend.

On the off chance a band toured through Eugene, there were two venues to play. The WOW Hall was where I saw most local shows growing up. Menomena, Joanna Newsom, Bill Callahan, Mount Eerie, and the Rock n Roll Soldiers, who were the closest band Eugene could claim as hometown heroes. They wore headbands and leather vests with tassels that hung over their bare chests, and we admired them because they were the only people we knew who had left and accomplished something—a coveted major-label deal and a slot in a Verizon Wireless commercial. We never stopped to question if what they'd accomplished had really been so great, why they were back in town to play so often.

Bigger bands played the McDonald Theatre, where I saw Modest Mouse and crowd surfed for the first time, spending a good thirty seconds on the edge of the stage beforehand to ensure someone in the front row would in fact catch me when I jumped. Isaac Brock was like a god to us. There was a rumor that his cousin lived in the next town over, in the trailer park that the song "Trailer Trash" is about, and this potential proximity made him all the more relatable—someone we could claim as our own. Everyone I knew had somehow memorized every word to his sprawling, hundred-track catalog, including the songs from his side projects and B-sides, coveted albums we were constantly trying to track down to burn and slip into the plastic sleeves of our CD binders. His lyrics epitomized what it felt like to grow up in a small gray town in the Pacific Northwest. What it was like to suffocate slowly from the boredom. His swelling eleven-minute opuses and cathartic, blood-curdling screams soundtracked every long drive with nothing to think about.

But nothing impacted me so profoundly as the first time I got my hands on a DVD of the Yeah Yeah Yeahs live at the Fillmore. The front woman, Karen O, was the first icon of the music world I worshipped who looked like me. She was half Korean and half white, with an unrivaled showmanship that obliterated the docile Asian stereotype. She was famous for wild onstage antics, spitting water into the air, bounding across to the far edges of the stage, and deep throating a microphone before lassoing it above her head by its cable. Agape at the image, I found myself in a strange state of ambivalence. My first thought being how do I get to do that, and my second, if there's already one Asian girl doing this, then there's no longer space for me.

Back then, I didn't know what a scarcity mentality was. The dialogue surrounding representation in music was in its nascent stages, and because I didn't personally know any other girls who played music, I didn't know there were others like me struggling with the same feelings. I didn't have the analogical capacity to imagine a white boy in the same situation, watching a live DVD of say, the Stooges, and thinking, if there's already an Iggy Pop, how could there possibly be room for another white guy in music?

Nevertheless, Karen O made music feel more accessible, made me believe it was possible that someone like me could one day make something that meant something to other people. Fueled by this newfound optimism, I began to badger my mother incessantly for a guitar. Having already sunk a hefty sum on a long list of extracurriculars I'd summarily abandoned, she was reluctant to oblige, but by Christmas she finally broke down, and at last I received a hundred-dollar Yamaha acoustic in a box from Costco.

The action was so high it felt like you had to wrestle the strings half an inch to pin them to the fret.

I started taking lessons once a week at the most embarrassing place one can learn how to play the guitar—the Lesson Factory. The Lesson Factory was like the Walmart of guitar lessons. It was connected to the Guitar Center and inside there were about ten soundproof cubicles, each equipped with two chairs and two amplifiers and your very own defeated musician recruited off Craigslist. I was lucky enough to be paired with a teacher I actually liked, who must have considered me a welcome break from prepubescent boys who exclusively wanted to learn how to play Green Day songs and the intro to "Stairway to Heaven."

The lessons couldn't have come at a better time. That same year Nick Hawley-Gamer took the seat next to me in English and it felt like I'd won the lottery. I'd heard about him because he was Maya Brown's neighbor and ex-boyfriend. I didn't have any classes with Maya, but she was known to all of us because every boy in our grade had a crush on her. Infuriatingly, she was objectively pretty and popular but masqueraded as a tormented alternative. She dyed her brown hair jet black, wore caramel-colored corduroys, and would write things on her arms in pen so she wouldn't forget them, thoughts she later wrote in her LiveJournal, which I followed assiduously even though we weren't friends in real life. Her entries were made up of Bright Eyes lyrics conflated with her own romantic encounters and meandering ruminations largely written in the second person, directed at someone anonymous who had either wronged her or for whom she desperately longed. I thought she was one of the great American poets of our time.

Nick had shaggy blond hair, painted his nails with Wite-Out, and wore a silver hoop earring in one ear. In class, he was quiet and terribly slow, like he was stoned all the time. He was constantly asking me when assignments were due and if he could borrow my notes, hapless requests that I deftly roped into my private mission to befriend him. In middle school Nick had a band called the Barrowites. I didn't know anyone who played in a band, and it felt impossibly cool that Nick already had one. They put out one EP before disbanding, which I diligently hunted down from a friend of a friend. It was a burned disc folded inside a homemade paper envelope with drawings and titles written in Sharpie. As soon as I got home I slipped the disc into the boom box I kept on my desk. I sat on a rolling chair and listened, still holding the paper envelope in my clammy hands as I pored over the lyrics, imagining Nick Hawley-Gamer's wildly sexually experienced past. There were five tracks, the last a song called "Molly's Lips." I wondered if Molly was another one of his many exes, or if it was perhaps a pseudonym for Maya Brown. I was too stupid to know that "Molly's Lips" was actually just a Nirvana cover, and I'd like to think that Nick was at least too stupid to know that Nirvana was covering the Vaselines.

Eventually I worked up enough courage to ask if he wanted to "jam." We met at lunch under a tree by the soccer fields. It didn't take long to reveal how horribly inept I was at the guitar. I had never "jammed" with anyone before. Nick would start a song and I'd have no idea what key it was in or how to accompany him. I tried to quietly hunt and peck for the right notes, attempting to hone in on a simple lead line vaguely rooted in the scales I thought I knew, before eventually apologizing and giving up completely. Nick took it in stride. He was patient and nonjudgmental and offered to play along instead to the songs I knew. We spent the rest of lunch trading verses on the White Stripes' "We're Going to Be Friends" and the Velvet Underground's "After Hours" and it felt like the most romantic miracle of my young adult life.

When I had written a few songs of my own, I decided to sign up for an open mic night at Cozmic Pizza, a restaurant downtown with café table seating and a small stage behind the front bar. It had glossy cement floors and high ceilings and usually hosted jazz nights and world music. I invited my friends to watch me play. The place was mostly empty, but still you could barely hear my Costco acoustic over the clanking of pint glasses, the slamming of the pizza oven, and the cashiers calling out names to collect their pies. I was elated by my seven minutes of fame. Because I'd brought a group of friends, the open mic slots slowly transformed into my own sets, opening for small local artists. I took press pictures of myself in my bathroom with a self-timer, scanned them onto my dad's computer, and used MS Paint to design promotional flyers. I bought a staple gun and hung them on telephone poles around town and asked local businesses if I could tape them up in their windows. I made a Myspace and uploaded the songs I recorded on GarageBand. I emailed the link to local bands and promoters and begged them to add me to their bills. I played high school benefits and developed a small local following, mostly of friends and class-mates I pressured into attendance, until finally I was "big enough" to land a slot at the WOW Hall opening for Maria Taylor.

On the day of the show, Nick came early for moral support and waited with me in the greenroom until it was time for my set. I'd never been in a greenroom before, but even so it hardly felt glam-orous. The room was brightly lit, closet-sized, with two benches and a mini fridge that sat atop a wooden table. Nick and I were sitting on a bench facing the door when Maria Taylor came in with a flannel-clad bandmate. She was intimidating. Dark, wavy hair framed her intense features, most recognizably her long, promi-nent nose and willowy figure. I held my breath as she entered. She mumbled, "Where's the wine?" and then left.

My parents came and stood together in the back. I played about six acoustic songs, seated on a metal fold-out chair, wearing a striped rainbow shirt from Forever 21 with faded flared jeans tucked into brown cowboy boots, an outfit I actually thought made me look cool at the time. By then, thank god, I had at least upgraded to a Taylor acoustic and played out of an SWR strawberry-blond amp I'd chosen solely because I liked the red-and-cream color combo. I fumbled through open chords, using a capo along the neck for each song so I could reuse the same chord shapes. I sang teenage songs about longing for the simpler times, not realizing that's exactly what these times were supposed to be. When I finished, I got a "Good job, sweetie" from my parents, who generously allowed me to hang around for the rest of the show.

Maria Taylor played a red Gretsch hollow body that looked comically large on her thin frame. I grabbed Nick's shoulder in excitement as she started the chords to "Xanax," the lead single off her new record that I'd been putting on all my mixes. The song started like a ticking clock, drumsticks clacking against the snare rim as she cataloged her anxieties and fears. "Afraid of an airplane, of a car swerving in the lane . . . of the icy mountain roads we have to take to get to the show." She jolted her torso forward into the last strum, and the members of the band, who'd stood stock-still through the entirety of the first two verses, collapsed in unison into the chorus.

Even as I sang along to a song that specifically addressed the constant challenges of life on tour, even as I watched them play to a small ridge of at best thirty people in a small town they probably regretted booking, witnessing someone who toured the country playing songs they wrote was a revelation. I'd shared a stage with this person, sat two feet away in the same room as them. I had glimpsed the life of an artist, and it felt, for a moment, like a path slightly more within reach.

After the show Nick gave me a ride home in his parents' Nissan Maxima. He was proud of me, and it felt good that someone I looked up to was seeing me in a new light.

"You should really record an album of all your songs," Nick

said. "You should look into the studio where we recorded the Barrowites."

THE NEXT MORNING, my mom took me to lunch at Seoul Cafe, the restaurant near the university run by a Korean couple. The husband worked the floor while the wife cooked in the back. Its only fault was that the service was slow, the husband easily flustered when he had more than three tables to deal with. As a work-around, my mother would call on the drive over about halfway between our house and the restaurant and phone in our orders in advance.

"Do you want bibimbap today?" she asked, holding the steering wheel with one hand and searching the contacts of her pink Razr flip phone with the other.

"Yeah, that sounds good."

"Ah ne! Ajeossi . . . ?"

Every time my mother spoke Korean, the text sprawled out before me like a Mad Lib. Words that were so familiar mixed with long blanks I couldn't fill in. I knew she was ordering jjamppong with extra vegetables, because I knew those words and because she always ordered the same thing. If she liked something, she stuck to it, ate it every day, seemingly never tiring of it, until one day she'd just move on inexplicably.

When we arrived, my mother greeted the old man at the counter with a big smile and burst into Korean while I dutifully poured hot tea for us from a large metal urn and placed our napkins, metal spoons, and chopsticks on the table. She paid at the counter, grabbed a Korean magazine from the front, and brought it back to our booth.

"I really like them here but they're very slow. That's why Mommy always call ahead," she whispered.

She flipped through the magazine, drinking her barley tea and taking in the Korean actresses and models. "I think maybe this would be nice hairstyle for you," she said, pointing at a Korean actress with perfectly neat, wavy tresses. She flipped the page again. "This kind of military jacket is very popular style in Korea now. Mommy want to get you one but you always wear ugly thing."

The old man wheeled our dishes over on a cart and placed our orders and banchan on the table. The rice at the bottom of my dolsot crackled and my mother's seafood noodle soup bellowed a steam bath from its bright red surface.

"Masitge deuseyo," the man said with a slight bow, wishing us a good meal as he pushed his cart back to the counter.

"What'd you think of my show yesterday?" I said, squirting gochujang into my bibimbap.

"Honey, don't put too much gochujang or it taste too salty," she said. She swatted my hand away from my bowl. I set down the red squeeze bottle with token obedience.

"Nick said he knows a studio where I could record my songs. I'm thinking since it's just guitar and vocals, I could record like an album in two or three days. It'd only be like two hundred dollars for the studio time, and then I could burn the discs at home."

My mother lifted up a long string of noodles, then let them drop back into the broth. She set her chopsticks across the top of the bowl, closed the magazine, and met my eyes across the table.

"I'm just waiting for you to give this up," she said.

My eyes fell into my rice. I broke my yolk with my spoon and pushed it around the stone bowl over the vegetables. My mother leaned in and began spooning some bean sprout soup into my bibimbap. The liquid sizzled against the sides.

"I should have never let you take guitar class," she said. "You should be thinking about the colleges, not doing this weird thing."

I bobbed my left leg up and down nervously, trying not to explode. My mother grabbed my thigh under the table.

"Stop shaking your leg; you'll shake the luck out."

"What if I don't want to go to college?" I said brazenly, wrenching away from her grasp. I shoveled a spoonful of the scalding mixed rice into my mouth, lobbing it around with my tongue, creating an air pocket that let out the steam. My mother looked around the restaurant nervously, as if I had just pledged faith to a satanic commune. I watched her try to collect herself.

"I don't care if you don't want to go to college. You have to go to college."

"You don't know me at all," I said. "This weird thing—is the thing that *I love*."

"Oh okay, fine then, you go live with Colette!" she erupted. She grabbed her purse and stood, sliding on her oversized sunglasses. "I'm sure she'll take care of you. You can do whatever you want there and I am so evil."

By the time I followed her out to the parking lot, she was already in the driver's seat, using the mirror from the sun flap to pick the gochugaru from her teeth with the folded corner of a receipt. She was waiting for me to stop her—to chase her and beg for forgiveness. But I would not give in. I could live without them, I thought to myself with foolish teenage confidence. I could get a job. I could stay with friends. I could keep playing shows until someday the rooms were full.

My mother crumpled the receipt into the cup holder, closed the mirror, and rolled down her window. I stood still in the parking lot, trying my best not to tremble as she stared me down from behind her dark lenses.

"You want to be a starving musician?" she said. "Then go live like one."

---

THE ALLURE OF LIFE as a starving musician wore off quickly. I stayed with Nicole and Colette a few nights, then with my friend Shanon, who was a year older and had her own place. We hung around at a punk house called the Flower Shop that was basically a glorified squat. Crust punks slept on the floors, hurled glass bottles off the roof into the street, and threw kitchen knives into the drywall when they were drunk.

Without my mother as an anchor, I strayed even further from the responsibilities we'd been arguing about over the past year. The college supplements I needed to complete remained half-finished documents on my father's desktop computer and I was pulled into a vicious cycle of truancy. I skipped classes, missed assignments, became ashamed I had gotten so far behind, and then kept skipping because I didn't want to be confronted by the teachers who cared about me. Many mornings I would just sit outside on campus, smoking cigarettes in the high school parking lot, unable to go inside. I fantasized about dying. Every object in the world seemed to become a tool for it. The freeway a place to get pummeled, five stories high enough to jump off. I saw bottles of glass cleaner and wondered how much I'd have to swallow; I thought of hanging myself with the little string that makes window blinds go up and down.

When my midterm report card revealed I was failing all my classes and that my GPA had plummeted, my mother scheduled a meeting with the college counselor and begged for help. Frantically, she gathered the necessary documents, including the scrapped writing supplements, and sent them out to the colleges I had previously shown interest in. When I finally returned home, I began to see a therapist who prescribed medication for some "emotional breathing room" and addressed a letter to accompany my college applications explaining that this shift in mood and performance had been indicative of a mental breakdown.

MY REMAINING MONTHS at home were scored by a fraught silence. My mother would drift from room to room rarely acknowledging my presence. When I opted not to attend senior prom, she offered little more than a passing remark, despite the fact we had picked out a dress together nearly a year beforehand.

I yearned for my mother to speak to me but tried to appear stoic, knowing full well my constitution was much weaker than hers. She seemed unfazed by our distance right up until the day I packed to leave for Bryn Mawr, when at last the silence was broken.

"When I was your age I would have died for a mom who bought me nice clothes," she said.

I was sitting cross-legged on the carpet, folding a pair of overalls stitched entirely out of plaid patches I'd bought from Goodwill. I set the overalls inside my bag, alongside my ugly sweater collection and an oversized Daniel Johnston shirt I had cut into a muscle tee.

"I always had to wear Nami's leftovers and then watch Eunmi get new ones by the time they got to her," she said. "On the East Coast everyone is going to think you are a homeless person."

"Well, I'm not like you," I said. "I have more important things to think about than the way that I look."

In one fell swoop, my mother gripped me by the hip and spun me around to strike my backside with her palm. It was not the first time my mother had hit me, but as I grew older and bigger, the punishment seemed more and more unnatural. At that point, I weighed more than her, and the strike hardly hurt, aside from the embarrassment of feeling much too old for the practice.

Hearing the commotion, my father made his way up the stairs and looked on from the hallway.

"Hit her!" my mother instructed. He stood still, watching dumbly. "Hit her!" she screamed again.

"If you hit me I'm going to call the police!"

My father grabbed me by the arm and raised his hand, but before he could bring it down, I wriggled out of his grasp, ran to the phone, and dialed 911.

My mother looked at me as if I were a worm, an unfamiliar speck eating away at all her efforts. This was not the girl who clung to her sleeves at the grocery store. This was not the girl who begged to sleep on the floor beside her bed. With the phone to my ear, I stared back at her defiantly, but when I heard a voice on the other end of the line I panicked and hung up. My mother took it as an opportunity to tackle me. She grabbed me by the forearms, and for the first time, we were locked together, wrestling to pin each other to the carpet. I tried to fight her off but discovered there was a physical place I would not go, a strength I knew I had to overtake her but could not access. I let her pin my wrists and climb on top of my stomach.

"Why are you doing this to us? After everything we have given you, how can you treat us this way?" she yelled, her tears and spit falling onto my face. She smelled like olive oil and citrus. Her hands felt soft and slick, greased with cream, as they pushed my wrists against the coarse carpet. The weight of her on me began to ache like a bruise. My father hovered over us, unsure of his place in it all, searching for a reason why a kid like me could wind up so miserable.

"I had an abortion after you because you were such a terrible child!"

Her grip went slack and she shifted her weight off me to leave the room. She let out a little cluck, the kind of sound let out when you think something is a real shame, like passing a dilapidated building with beautiful architecture.

There it was. It was almost comical how she could have with-held a secret so impressive my entire life, only to hurl it at such a moment. I knew there was no way I was truly to blame for the abortion. That she had said it just to hurt me as I had hurt her in so many monstrous configurations. More than anything, I was just shocked she had withheld something so monumental.

I envied and feared my mother's ability to keep matters private, as every secret I tried to hold close ate away at me. She possessed a rare talent for keeping secrets, even from us. She did not need anyone. She could surprise you with how little she needed you. All those years she instructed me to save 10 percent of myself like she did, I never knew it meant she had also been keeping a part of herself from me too.

# 6

## Dark Matter

This could be my chance, I thought, to make amends for everything. For all the burdens I'd imposed as a hyperactive child, for all the vitriol I'd spewed as a tortured teen. For hiding in department stores, throwing tantrums in public, destroying her favorite objects. For stealing the car, coming home on mushrooms, drunk driving into a ditch.

I would radiate joy and positivity and it would cure her. I would wear whatever she wanted, complete every chore without protest. I would learn to cook for her—all the things she loved to eat, and I would singlehandedly keep her from withering away. I would repay her for all the debts I'd accrued. I would be everything she ever needed. I would make her sorry for ever not wanting me to be there. I would be the perfect daughter.

OVER THE COURSE of the next two weeks my father was able to arrange an appointment at MD Anderson and my parents flew to

Houston. With better imaging, they discovered my mother did not have pancreatic cancer but a rare form of stage IV squamous-cell carcinoma that had likely originated in the bile duct. The doctors told them if they had moved forward with the surgery the first doctor suggested, she would have bled out on the operating table. The recommended course of action now was to return home and hit it with a three-drug Molotov cocktail, then follow up with radiation if the results were positive. My mom was only fifty-six and despite the cancer, relatively healthy. They felt if they went in strong, there was a possibility she could still beat it.

Back in Eugene my mother sent me a photo of her new pixie cut. She'd had the same hairstyle for more than ten years, simple, straight, and falling just below her shoulders. Sometimes she'd wear it in a loose ponytail, often with a visor or a sun hat in the summer, a beanie or a little newsboy cap in the fall. Aside from the perm she had when she was younger, I'd never seen it styled any other way. "It suits you!" I messaged back ecstatically, following up with a number of enamored, animated emojis. "You look younger!!! Mia Farrow!!!" I meant it. In the photo she was smiling, posing in front of a white wall in the living room, near the kitchen counter where my parents kept their car keys and the landline. There was a plastic port on her chest, its edges secured with clear medical tape. She looked almost coy. Her expression was hopeful, her posture slightly bent, and it made me hopeful too.

IN SPITE of my mother's initial objections, I quit my three jobs, sublet my apartment, and put the band on hiatus. My plan was to spend the summer in Eugene and return to Philadelphia in August for our two-week tour. By then I would have a better idea of what my family and I were in for, and whether or not I should move out indefinitely. In the interim, Peter would visit.

I landed in Eugene in the afternoon, the day after my mother's first chemotherapy infusion. I'd done my best to look poised and put together, spending my layover at the San Francisco airport in front of the women's room mirror. I washed my face in the sink and dabbed it dry with a rough paper towel. I brushed my hair and reapplied my makeup, cautiously lining my lids with the thinnest flick of a cat eye I could manage. I took the lint roller out of my carry-on and rolled the sticky paper over my jeans and picked at the pills on my sweater. I smoothed the wrinkles as best I could with the palms of my hands. I put more effort into composing myself for my mother than I had for any date or job interview.

I had prepared for our visits this way since college, when I'd return home for winter and summer breaks. In December of my freshman year, I carefully polished a pair of cowboy boots she sent me, dipping a soft cloth into the waxy paste they came with and running it over the leather, blending it in small circles with the bristles of a wooden brush.

Though my mother and I hadn't parted on good terms, once a month, huge boxes would arrive, reminders I was never far from her mind. Sweet honey-puffed rice, twenty-four packs of individually wrapped seasoned seaweed, microwavable rice, shrimp crackers, boxes of Pepero, and cups of Shin ramen I would subsist on for weeks on end in an effort to avoid the dining hall. She sent clothing steamers, lint rollers, BB creams, packages of socks. A new "this is nice brand" skirt she'd found on sale at T. J. Maxx. The cowboy boots arrived in one of these packages after my parents had vacationed in Mexico. When I slipped them on I discovered they'd already been broken in. My mother had worn them around the house for a week, smoothing the hard edges in two pairs of socks for an hour every day, molding the flat sole with the bottom of her feet, wearing in the stiffness, breaking the tough leather to spare me all discomfort.

I stood before the full-length mirror in my dorm room and scanned myself for errors, scouring my outfit for snags and loose threads. I tried to see myself through my mother's shrewd eye, pinpoint the parts of me she'd pick apart. I wanted to impress her, to demonstrate how much I'd grown and how I could thrive without her. I wanted to return an adult.

My mother prepared for our reunions in her own way, marinating short rib two days before my arrival. She filled the fridge with my favorite side dishes and bought my favorite radish kimchi weeks in advance, leaving it out on the counter for a day so it was extra fermented and tart by the time I got home.

Tender short rib, soused in sesame oil, sweet syrup, and soda and caramelized in the pan, filled the kitchen with a rich, smoky scent. My mother rinsed fresh red-leaf lettuce and set it on the glass-top coffee table in front of me, then brought the banchan. Hard-boiled soy-sauce eggs sliced in half, crunchy bean sprouts flavored with scallions and sesame oil, doenjang jjigae with extra broth, and chonggak kimchi, perfectly soured.

Julia, the golden retriever we'd had since I was twelve, fell onto her back, paws up, submitting her giant stomach in a pose my mother always referred to as "breasts up!" while my mother grilled the galbi I would always associate with the taste of home.

"Julia is getting fat," I said, running my hand over her protruding belly. "You're feeding her too much."

"I only give her dog food . . . and just a little bit of rice! She's a Korean dog; she loves her rice!"

Blissfully I laid my palm flat, blanketed it with a piece of lettuce, and dressed it just the way I liked—a piece of glistening short rib, a spoonful of warm rice, a dredge of ssamjang, and a thin slice of raw garlic. I folded it into a perfect little satchel and popped it into my mouth. I closed my eyes and savored the first few chews, my taste buds and stomach having been deprived for months of a home-cooked meal. The rice alone was a miraculous reunion, the cooker having imbued each kernel with textural autonomy, distinguishing it from the gluey, microwavable bowls I'd been surviving on in my dorm room. My mother lingered to take in my expression.

"Tastes good? Masisseo?" She opened a package of seaweed and placed it next to my rice bowl.

"Jinjja masisseo!" I said, my mouth still half-full, fainting in dramatic appreciation.

My mother sat behind me on the couch, pushing my hair behind my shoulders and out of my face as I gorged ravenously on the bounties of the feast. It was a familiar touch, her cool and sticky hand smoothed with cream, one I found myself no longer lurching away from but leaning into. It was as if I possessed a new internal core that gravitated toward her affection, its charge renewed by the time I'd spent away from its field. I found myself eager to please her again, savoring the laughter she broke into as I regaled her with stories about confronting adulthood, drawing out the details of my ineptitude. How I'd shrunk a sweater two sizes in the wash, how I'd taken myself out to a fancy lunch and accidentally spent twelve dollars on sparkling water, thinking it was complimentary. Admissions that surrendered, Mom, you were right.

AS I DESCENDED the escalator of the Eugene airport, I half expected my mother to be waiting for me like she used to, alone in the terminal just beyond security, waving as I came into view. She'd always be there to get me, dressed neatly in all black with a large faux fur vest and huge tortoiseshell sunglasses, looking out of place among the other residents of Eugene in their baggy green Oregon Ducks hoodies.

Instead, I found my father outside, parked by the baggage claim exit.

"Hey, bud," he said. He gave me a hug and lifted my suitcase into the trunk.

"How's she doing?"

"She's okay. She went in for the chemo yesterday. Says she just feels a little weak."

We were quiet in the car and I rolled down the window to take a deep breath of Oregon air. It was warm and smelled like cut grass and the beginning of summer. We drove past the long stretch of empty fields, then the big-box stores on the outskirts of town, past the home of a best friend I no longer knew, repainted now, the lawn fenced in.

Per usual, my dad drove aggressively, weaving in and out of traffic at odds with the naturally slow pace of the small college town. It felt strange to be together without my mother. The two of us never spent much time alone.

My father was happy as a provider. His mere existence in our lives was testament enough to how he'd transcended his own upbringing and overcome his addictions, and that counted for something.

As a kid I was enthralled with the stories of his past, his machismo and grit. He would regale me with the fights of his youth, sparing no detail. How he'd once blinded a man, how he'd been held at knifepoint, how he'd stayed up for twenty-three days on a speed bender living under the boardwalk. He rode a Harley and wore an earring and his stockiness always made me feel safe and protected. And he could drink. After work he'd hold court at the Highlands, a local bar across from his office. He could knock back shots of tequila and a half-dozen beers like it was nothing and the next morning appear completely unscathed.

Unlike my mother, he tried to raise me with indifference to gender, teaching me how to ball a fist and how to build a fire. When

I was ten he even bought me my own Yamaha 80cc motorbike so I could follow him along the muddy circuit in the backyard.

But for most of my childhood he was away at work or at the bar, and when he was home, most of his time was spent roaring into the phone, looking for a missing pallet of strawberries or trying to find out why a truckload of romaine was running three days behind. Over time our conversations became a lot like explaining a movie to someone who has walked in on the last thirty minutes.

My father often blamed his work for the distance that grew between us. I was ten when he took over his brother's business and his workload practically doubled. But the truth was his new position coincided with the purchase of our family's first desktop computer, which was when I first stumbled across the paid affairs he'd been scheduling with women online. It was a secret I kept from my mother my entire life.

Even at a young age I was quick to rationalize my father's infidelity. He was a man with needs and I assumed my parents must have come to some sort of understanding. But as I grew older the secret began to fester. The same stories grew tiresome and repetitive, his violent past less the exploits of a hero than excuses for his shortcomings. His constant lack of sobriety was no longer endearing; the drunk driving after work, irresponsible. What had been a delight as a child fell short of what I needed from a father as an adult. We were not innately, intrinsically intertwined the way I was with my mother, and now that she was sick, I was unsure of how we'd manage to pull through together.

WE HEADED UP Willamette Street, clearing the steep hill that passed the sloping cemetery. The pavement changed where a sign marked the end of city limits and a sequence I'd seen a thousand times unfurled. There still were the same bends where deer were likely to jump, the straightaways where my dad would try to pass slow-moving Volvos and Subarus headed up to Spencer Butte. Then the winding stretch of guardrail and the clearing, where hills of yellowing grass opened west to the uninterrupted sunset. Up and up, the pines taking over, obscuring the houses behind them, past the butte and Duckworth's Nursery, where peacocks roamed freely through the groves of potted trees and shrubs, past the Christmas-tree farm on Fox Hollow Road, and down the gravel path covered by a canopy of trees and ferns and moss all growing into one another like a lattice until the lush mass broke open to our home.

Dad parked the car and I hurried inside, lining my shoes up neatly in the mudroom. I called out to her as I entered through the kitchen, and she stood up from the couch.

"Hello, my baby!" she called back to me.

I went to her, embracing her cautiously. I felt the hard plastic port between us. I ran my hand over her hair.

"It looks so good," I said. "I love it."

She sat back down and I slinked off the leather couch and sat on the rug between her and the coffee table. Julia panted beside us, her tongue lobbing over the missing canine my father had accidentally knocked out a few years ago, driving golf balls off the driveway tee. I hugged my mother's calves and leaned my head on her lap. I had expected our reunion to be emotional, but she seemed calm and unmoved.

"How do you feel?"

"I feel fine," she said. "I feel a little weak, but I feel fine."

"You have to eat a lot to keep your health up. I want to learn how to make all the Korean dishes you like."

"Oh yes, you becoming such a good cook from the picture you been sending me. Tomorrow morning how about you make me some fresh tomato juice? I buy two or three organic tomatoes and I blend it in the Vitamix with some honey and ice. Taste so good. Lately I've been making that one."

"Tomato juice. Got it."

"In two weeks Mommy's friend Kye is going to come. And then maybe she can teach you how to make some Korean foods."

Kye was my mother's friend from my parents' time in Japan. She was a few years older than my mother and had taken her under her wing while my father worked the used car lots in Misawa. She showed her where to shop, where to drink, how to drive, and how to side hustle, black-marketing items from the PX, the discount department store on base where the GIs did their shopping. Coffee creamer, dish soap, fifths of foreign booze, tins of Spam—my mom would buy these rarities tax-free from the PX for a buck and flip them for five.

They had lost touch after my parents moved to Germany but reconnected a couple of years ago. She lived in Georgia now with her husband, Woody. I'd never met her and I was excited to learn from her, to prove to my mother how useful I could be. I fantasized about the delicious food we'd make together, finally repaying my debts, giving back some of the love and care I'd taken for granted for so many years. Dishes that would comfort her and remind her of Korea. Meals prepared just the way she liked them, to lift her spirits and nourish her body and give her the strength she'd need to recover.

WE WATCHED TELEVISION together for a while, quietly picking the thistles out of Julia's fur and searching for ticks to burn while she panted on her side, pawing at our wrists, hungry for attention every time our eyes drifted away from her and toward the screen. My mother went to bed early and I brought my bag upstairs.

My bedroom was above my parents', a wide rectangle tapering into little alcoves with the hips of the roof on either side. My desk was nestled into one niche, my record player cabinet and speakers and a blue-cushioned window seat in the other. The alcoves were painted bright tangerine and the middle section mint, loudly proclaiming from the upper corner of the house: teenage girl was here.

"Stop making all that hole!" my mother would scold from the staircase as I nailed psychedelic tapestries to my ceiling and pinned gigantic Janis Joplin and *Star Wars* posters to my wall. I found the old record player cabinet and its hideous wooden speakers at Goodwill. "We can paint it!" I said, thrilled at the idea of sharing a creative project with my mother. But once we got them back to the house, I was left to my own devices. I laid out newspaper in the garage and spray-painted the cabinets black and, too impatient to let them dry properly, immediately set in on large white polka dots, which of course dripped and became misshapen, rendering the impression of a melting cow. It reminded me of many such half-baked teenage failures, underscoring the point when I put an old Leonard Cohen album on and remembered that it only played in mono.

I opened the window, the screen of which I'd removed and stashed in a storage closet years ago, and climbed onto the roof. I leaned against the coarse tar paper, setting my feet above the gutter and steadying myself on the slope. There were so many stars out, more brilliant than I'd even remembered, uncorrupted by the lights of the city. The sounds of crickets and frogs resonated from below. At the other end of the roof, when my parents were sleeping, I used to slide down the columns of the portico and meet with whichever kid I'd enlisted to drive for the night. Outside, I'd bound up the gravel driveway to my liberators, engines idling, and I was free.

There wasn't much to do when we snuck out. Most of the time, the kids who picked me up weren't even particularly close friends, just bored classmates or older kids with licenses who were still awake with nothing else to do. Every so often there'd be a rave in the woods and we'd dress in elaborate costumes and dance along with the anonymous hippies on ecstasy. Sometimes I would pilfer liquor left over from my parents' holiday parties and, like a careful chemist, siphon from the various bottles inconspicuous levels of liquid to mix with soda and drink in the park. But most of the time we'd just drive around listening to CDs, occasionally venturing as far as an hour out to Dexter Reservoir or Fern Ridge just to sit on the dock and look out at the black water, dark as oil in the night, a bleak expanse we'd use as a sounding board for how confused we were about ourselves and what exactly it was that we were feeling. Other nights we'd drive up to Skinner Butte to get a good view of the dull city that kept us hostage or drink coffee and eat grated hash browns at the twenty-four-hour IHOP, or sneak our way through some stranger's acreage where we'd once discovered a rope swing. Once we even drove out to the airport just to watch people at the terminal, flying off to cities where we desperately wished we could travel, a couple of nocturnal teens bonded together by a deep, inexplicable loneliness and AOL instant messenger.

It was not lost on me how different the circumstances were now. Here I was again, this time returned of my own free will, no longer scheming a wild escape into the dark but desperately hoping that a darkness would not come in.

# 7

# Medicine

The first couple of days were quiet and still. We kept waiting to see what would happen, as if something sinister were looming, slowly stalking the perimeter of the house. But for the first few days, she felt fine. I figured, three days in already, maybe it wouldn't be so bad after all.

Each morning I washed and cut three organic tomatoes and blended them together with honey and ice as she'd instructed. Other meals proved more challenging. I didn't know how to cook many Korean dishes on my own, and the few I had learned to prepare were too heavy for her current state. I felt lost. I asked her constantly if she could think of anything I could cook for her, but she had no cravings to chase and dismissed my suggestions listlessly. The only thing she could come up with was Ottogi brand cream soup, an instant powder I could buy at the Asian grocery that was neutral and easy to digest.

There was no H Mart in Eugene. Instead, twice a week my mother and I would go shopping for Korean groceries at Sunrise

Market, a small business in town run by a Korean family. The husband was short and dark. He wore large aviator glasses and yellow work gloves and was constantly winded from hauling new shipments inside. The wife was pretty and petite and wore her hair in a short perm. She was friendly and soft-spoken and usually worked the register. Occasionally, one of their three daughters would be there to help bag groceries and stock the shelves. Every few years a new daughter would grow old enough to replace whichever one went off to school, and I would hear the name of some prestigious college proudly mentioned, poking out of the Korean phrases she exchanged with my mother, ringing up our bean sprouts and tofu.

At the front of the store there were giant sacks of rice piled high on industrial shelving that wrapped around to an open refrigerator with ten different types of kimchi and banchan. There were aisles of instant noodles and curries in the center, freezers full of mixed seafood and dumplings on the other edge. In the back corner there was a Korean VHS section with shelves full of bootleg tapes housed in anonymous white sleeves, handwritten texts running down their spines, where my mom would rent outdated series of K-dramas her friends and family in Seoul had already seen and had been telling her about for years. If I was good, my mother would treat me to a snack displayed near the register, usually a Yakult yogurt drink or a little cup of fruit jelly, or the two of us might share a package of mochi on the drive home.

When I was nine, Sunrise Market relocated to a larger store. My mom pored giddily over the new imports that came with the expansion: pollack roe frozen in little wooden boxes; packages of Chapagetti instant black-bean noodles; bungeo-ppang, fish-shaped pastry filled with ice cream and sweet red-bean paste, each new item reviving bygone memories of her childhood, conjuring new recipes to capture old tastes.

It was strange to be on my own in a place we'd always gone to together. I was so accustomed to following her lead as she investigated frozen bags of mixed seafood and pajeon flour mix, likely trying to discern which was most similar to the ones Halmoni would use. Untethered from my mother's cart, I scanned the shelves for the instant soup she'd asked me to find, slowly reading the Korean characters in search of the correct brand.

I learned to read and write Korean in Korean language school, Hangul Hakkyo. Every Friday from first to sixth grade, my mother would take me to the Korean Presbyterian Church. A small building at the bottom of the parking lot housed two or three classrooms separated into varying levels of difficulty. The rooms were all covered in colorful illustrations of Bible scenes left over from Sunday school. Up the hill was a larger building with a kitchen and another classroom, and upstairs the actual church where we gathered for assemblies once or twice a year.

Every week the mothers would take turns providing dinner. While some approached this service piously, an opportunity to prepare traditional Korean fare, others regarded it as a rote duty and were perfectly content to order ten boxes of Little Caesars, much to the delight of the students. "I can't believe they actually like pizza for dinner when Grace's umma was just being lazy," my mother would grumble on the ride home. All the Korean moms took on the names of their children. Jiyeon's mom was Jiyeon's umma. Esther's mom was Esther's umma. I never learned any of their real names. Their identities were absorbed by their children.

When it was my mom's turn she made gimbap. At home after school she cooked a big pot of rice and spent hours rolling yellow pickled radish, carrots, spinach, beef, and sliced omelet into perfect cylinders with a thin bamboo mat, then cut them into colorful, bite-sized coins. Before class the two of us snacked on the leftover ends where the vegetables protruded messily out of the sides.

I didn't have any Korean friends outside of Hangul Hakkyo. During our dinner breaks, I often felt out of place, wandering around the parking lot, which doubled as a playground for our half-hour recess. There was a basketball hoop that the older boys would commandeer. Everyone else just sat on the curbs trying to entertain themselves. Most of the kids there were full Korean, and I struggled to relate to the obedience that seemed to possess them, inculcated by the united force of two immigrant parents. They wore the visors their moms bought for them without protest and all attended church together on Sundays, a practice my mother had opted out of early on, despite the central role Christianity seemed to play in our sparse Korean community. Perhaps by nature of my mixed upbringing, I always felt like the bad kid, which only made me act out more. When I misbehaved, the teachers would make me stand in the corner with my arms over my head while the others carried on with their lessons. I never became fluent in Korean, but I did manage to learn to read and write.

"KEU-REEM SEU-PEU," I said quietly, sounding out the Konglish. For someone like me who was just barely literate, Konglish was a blessed free pass to a large bank of vocabulary. It's a fusion of Korean and English that obeys Korean rules of pronunciation. Since there is no *z* in the Hangul alphabet, English words that contain the letter *z* get replaced with a *j* sound, so *pizza* becomes *pee-jah*, *amazing* becomes *ama-jing*, and a word like *cheese*, in which the *s* emulates a *z* sound, becomes *chee-jeu*. In this case, *r*'s were replaced with *l* sounds. "Keu-reem seu-peu," I whispered. Cream soup. The packet was bright orange and yellow and had a logo of a winking cartoon man licking his lips. I bought several varieties and a few bowls of the same brand's instant Korean porridge and a package of mochi and returned home.

I washed my hands and placed a pink mochi on a small plate to bring to her in bed.

"No thank you, honey," she said. "I don't feel like it."

"Come on, Mom. Just eat half of one."

I sat beside her, watching. She took a small bite unhappily and put it back on the plate, flicking the fine residue of sweet rice flour from her fingers before setting it on her nightstand. I left the room to prepare the cream soup.

I combined the dry powder with three cups of water and heated it through. I tried to recall some of the caretaking tips I'd read online. Serve small amounts frequently, create a pleasant mealtime atmosphere. Meals can be made more appealing if they're served in large bowls, making portions appear smaller and more manageable. I poured the contents into a pretty blue bowl big enough to make the soup seem like a drop in a well. Despite the illusion, she consumed only a few spoonfuls.

Later that evening, I had the brilliant idea of making gyeranjjim, a steamed, savory egg custard usually served as a side dish at Korean restaurants bringing their A game. Nutritious with a mild and soothing flavor, it was one of my favorites growing up.

I looked up a recipe online. I cracked four eggs into a small bowl and beat them with a fork. I searched the kitchen cabinets, found one of my mother's earthenware pots, and heated it over the stove, adding the beaten eggs, salt, and three cups of water. I put the lid on and after fifteen minutes returned to find it had come out perfectly soft and jiggly, like a pale yellow, silken tofu.

I set it on a hot pad on the table and eagerly helped my mother to the kitchen.

"I made gyeranjjim!"

My mother winced at the sight of it. She turned her face away with distaste.

"Oh no, baby," she said. "I really don't want this one right now."

I tried to temper my frustration, transform my disappointment into the anxious patience of a new mother with a colicky infant. How often must my mother have negotiated with and maneuvered around my infantile pickiness?

"Umma, I made it for you," I said. "You have to at least try it, just like you always taught me."

I was able to coax her into only a single bite before she retreated back to bed.

On the morning of the fourth day my mother became nauseous and threw up for the first time. I couldn't help but selfishly envision all my hard work flushed down the drain. I tried to keep her hydrated, insisting she drink water throughout the day, but every hour she rushed back to the bathroom, unable to keep anything down. By four o'clock I discovered her curled over the toilet, pushing her fingers down her throat in search of relief. My father and I pulled her up together and brought her back to bed. We scolded her, saying if she didn't work harder to try to keep food down, she wouldn't get better.

In the evening I called Seoul Cafe and phoned in an order of tteokguk, rice cake soup served in a mild beef broth. I figured if she wouldn't eat anything I made, maybe something from her favorite restaurant could entice her. At home, I ladled it out into another enormous bowl and brought it to her in bed. Again she resisted, managing only a few bites, which she vomited later that night.

We hoped we'd hit the peak of her side effects, but the next day was even worse. Depleted, she became too weak to leave her bed for the bathroom, and I'd have to rush to her bedside with the heart-shaped pink plastic bucket that held my bath toys when I was a child. Often by the time I rinsed it out in the tub, I'd have to run back to use it again. By the sixth day, her condition began to feel abnormal. She was scheduled for a checkup with the oncologist in the afternoon and we decided to bring her in early.

This was when we realized my mother had lost her mind. She couldn't stand on her own. She couldn't speak and only moaned softly, rocking back and forth as if she were hallucinating. Together, my father and I brought her to the car, wrapping her arms around our necks to support her weight. We propped her up in the passenger seat and I sat in the back while he drove. I watched her eyes roll back. It was as if her person had disappeared completely and she was entering another mental plane. In an effort to escape whatever hell she was enduring, she began to claw violently at the door to try to break free. My father howled for her to stop. He struggled to steer with one hand as he barred his other arm across her.

"Pull over!" I cried, terrified she'd wrestle out of his grip and tumble onto the pavement.

My father carried her to the back seat, where I pulled her in from beneath her arms. I laid her body over mine and held her as she moaned and wriggled against me, trying to reach for a way out. When we finally arrived at the oncology clinic, they took one look at her and told us we needed to head directly to the ER.

At Riverbend Hospital my father hooked his arms around her shoulders and pulled her into a wheelchair. Two men in blue scrubs at the front desk told us to take a seat in the waiting room. There were no rooms available. They glanced without sympathy at my mother and me as I tried to keep her from falling out of the wheelchair. She was moaning and rocking and extending her arms outward as if she were fighting against an invisible force. My father slammed the palms of his hands against the front desk.

"LOOK AT HER—SHE IS GOING TO DIE HERE IF YOU DON'T HELP US."

He looked rabid. A white foam formed at the corners of his lips, and I thought for a moment he might reach over and hit one of them.

"There!" I said, eyeing an empty room. "That room is empty! Please!"

They relented and let us take the room. After what felt like an eternity, the doctor finally arrived. My mother was dehydrated, and from what I can remember, her magnesium and potassium levels were dangerously low. She'd have to stay overnight. Nurses wheeled her away on a hospital bed to a new room upstairs, where they hooked her up to a series of IVs to stabilize her condition. My father sent me home to gather some of her things for the night.

BY THE TIME I LEFT it was already dark. Alone in the privacy of the car I finally let the shock melt away into tears. Everything I had ever done in my life felt so monumentally selfish and insignificant. I hated myself for not writing to Eunmi every day she was sick, for not calling more, for not comprehending what Nami Emo had endured as a caretaker. I hated myself for not arriving in Eugene earlier, for not being at the appointments, for not knowing the signs to look out for, and perhaps desperate to shirk responsibility, my hatred seeped toward my father and the warnings he'd failed to heed, the suffering that could have been avoided if we had just brought her to the hospital when the symptoms first began to appear.

I wiped my face with my sleeve and rolled the windows down. It was the first week of June and the breeze was warm. The moon was a luminescent little cuticle, my mother's favorite crescent shape. I used to mock her every time she said it, telling her it was an arbitrary preference when there were only three phases from which to pick. I took I-5 past Lane Community College and sped up on Willamette. I tried to shift my thoughts and focus on the road ahead, looking out for deer along the bends.

At home I grabbed a soft throw from the living room; my

mother's lotions, cleanser, toner, serum, and ChapStick from the bathroom counter; a soft gray cardigan from her closet. I packed an overnight bag for myself and new clothes for her to wear once we were allowed to leave. When I returned to Riverbend, my mother was sleeping. My father suggested we go back to the house together, but I couldn't stand the thought of her waking up alone in the hospital, confused as to how she'd even gotten there. I told him to go get some rest and come back in the morning, and I stretched out on the padded bench by the window.

That night, lying beside her, I remembered how when I was a child I would slip my cold feet between my mother's thighs to warm them. How she'd shiver and whisper that she would always suffer to bring me comfort, that that was how you knew someone really loved you. I remembered the boots she'd broken in so that by the time I got them I could go on unbothered, without harm. Now, more than ever, I wished desperately for a way to transfer pain, wished I could prove to my mother just how much I loved her, that I could just crawl into her hospital cot and press my body close enough to absorb her burden. It seemed only fair that life should present such an opportunity to prove one's filial piety. That the months my mother had been a vessel for me, her organs shifting and cramping together to make room for my existence, and the agony she'd endured upon my exit could be repaid by carrying this pain in her place. The rite of an only daughter. But I could do no more than lie nearby, ready to be her advocate, listening to the slow and steady beeping of machinery, the soft sounds of her breathing in and out.

IT TOOK DAYS for my mother to speak again. She remained in the hospital for two weeks. My father stayed with her during the day and I would stay with her in the evenings and overnight.

This new working order did not bode well for my father. He had the luxury of taking time off to help my mother through her treatment, but he was not a natural caretaker; a fateful challenge, perhaps, for a man who was not raised with the privilege of being cared for.

He had never met his own father, who'd been a paratrooper in the Second World War. Supposedly, on a crash-landing over Guam, his parachute got caught in a tree and he was stuck up there for days, witness to the slaughter of his entire unit before he was finally rescued. He returned a completely different person. He beat his children. He made them kneel on glass and threw salt in their wounds. He raped his wife, impregnating her with my father. She finally left him, just before my father was born.

Raised by a single working mother who hardly had the time or emotional capacity for the youngest of four, my father grew up without much supervision. His older siblings Gayle and David were ten and eleven years older, respectively, and already out of the house by the time he reached elementary school. Ron, who was six years his senior, perpetuated the abuses he'd endured onto my father, boxing him into unconsciousness and slipping him tabs of acid when my father was only nine, just to see what would happen.

A predictably troubled adolescence followed, culminating in his arrest, rehab and, a handful of relapses thereafter while he worked as an exterminator in his early twenties. It was his fortuitous move abroad that ultimately saved him. If this were my father's memoir, it'd probably be titled *The Greatest Used Car Salesman in the World*. More than thirty years later, nothing excites him more than talking about his years on the military base, working his way through the ranks of the company in Misawa, Heidelberg, and Seoul. For a man who came from nothing, life as a used car salesman abroad was a most glamorous calling.

These were the years my father seized the American dream in

a foreign country. While he may have been a man with few skills and little education, he could make up for it twice over in pure resilience and die-hard conviction. There was nothing he was too proud for—whatever it took, he was going to be the last one standing.

He took this newfound discipline with him back to Eugene, where he became a successful broker who relished attacking problems and delegating tasks. After a quarter life of failure, he finally found something he was good at, and he gave it everything. Part of that sacrifice meant he lived the life of a greyhound—eyes ahead, smell the blood, and fucking run.

But my mother's illness was not a problem he could negotiate his way out of or outwork after hours. And so he began to feel helpless, and then he began to run away.

I returned home at noon one day, groggy and exhausted from another night spent on the hospital bench, to find him seated at the kitchen table. The house smelled like burning.

"This isn't me," he muttered to himself. He was looking over his car insurance, shaking his head. He held the phone to his ear, waiting to settle the second fender bender he'd gotten into that week, for both of which he had been at fault. In the trash can were two pieces of blackened toast; in the toaster another was beginning to smoke.

I popped the toaster and took a butter knife to scrape some of the burnt bits into the sink. I put it on a plate and set it next to him on the table.

"I'm not like this," he said.

That night, before I left for the hospital, I found him in the same spot drifting in and out of sleep, mumbling incoherently. He was wearing an undershirt and a pair of white briefs.

It was nine o'clock and he had already polished off two bottles of wine and was sucking on one of the marijuana candies he'd bought from the dispensary for my mother.

"She can't even look at me," he said, beginning to blubber. "We can't even look at each other without crying."

His big body heaved up and down. The chapped crevices in his lips were inked dark purple with wine. It wasn't rare to see my father cry. He was a sensitive guy, despite his grit. He did not know how to withhold any part of his truth. Unlike my mother, he saved no 10 percent.

"You have to promise you're going to be there for me," he said. "Promise me, okay?"

He reached out for me and held on to my wrist, searching for my reassurance with his eyes half-open. In his other hand he was holding a half-eaten slice of Jarlsberg that folded limply over as he leaned toward me. I fought the urge to rip my arm away from him. I knew I should be feeling sympathy or empathy, camaraderie or compassion, but I only burned with resentment.

He was an undesirable partner in a game with the highest of stakes and insurmountable odds. He was my father and I wanted him to soberly reassure me, not try to goad me into navigating this disheartening path alone. I could not even cry in his presence for fear he would take the moment over, pit his grief against mine in a competition of who loved her more, and who had more to lose. Moreover, it shook me to my core that he had said aloud what I considered to be unspeakable. The possibility that she couldn't make it, that there could even be an us without her.

TWO WEEKS LATER, my mother was finally able to return home. I set up a space heater in the bathroom and ran her a bath, checking the water frequently to get it to the perfect temperature. I helped her from her bed slowly toward the tub. She was feeble and walked as if she were relearning how. I pulled down her pajama pants and lifted her shirt like she did for me when I was a child. "Man seh," I joked, something she used to say when undressing me, an instruction to raise my arms above my head.

I braced her weight on my shoulder and helped her step into the tub. I reminded her of the jjimjilbang, of the bet she'd won, how uncomfortable Peter and Dad must have been, sitting naked together. I told her it was lucky we already felt so comfortable with each other. That there were families who were embarrassed by nudity. I washed her black hair carefully, trying my best to rinse it clean without touching her hair at all, fearful it would break off in my hands.

"Look at my veins," she said, examining her stomach through the water. "Isn't it scary? They look black. Even when I was pregnant my body didn't look this weird. It's like there's poison in me."

"Medicine," I corrected her. "Killing all the bad things."

I unplugged the drain and helped her out of the tub, patting her down with a plush yellow towel. I worked as quickly as possible, trying to make sure she wouldn't fall. "Lean on me," I said, wrapping her in a fleece robe.

As the water drained, I noticed a black residue collecting along the sides of the white tub, ebbing with the surface of the water. When I looked back at my mother, her head was patchy. Large clumps of hair were missing from sections, revealing portions of her pale scalp. Torn between helping her stand and rushing to the tub to rinse away the evidence, I was too slow to keep my mother from catching a glimpse of herself in the full-length mirror. I could feel her body go limp, sliding down onto the carpet and out of my arms like sand.

She sat on the floor and confronted the reflection. She ran a hand along her head and stared at the hair that broke off into it.

In the same full-length mirror where I had watched her pose for more than half my life. The same mirror where I'd watched her apply cream after cream to preserve her taut, flawless skin. The same mirror where I'd find her trying on outfit after outfit, runway walking with perfect posture, examining herself with pride, posing with a new purse or leather jacket. The mirror where she lingered in all her vanity. In the mirror now there was someone unrecognizable and out of her control. Someone strange and undesirable. She started to cry.

I crouched down beside her and wrapped my arms around her shaking body. I wanted to cry with her, at this image I too did not recognize, this giant physical manifestation of evil that had entered our lives. But instead I felt my body stiffen, my heart harden, my feelings freeze over. An internal voice commanded, "Do not break down. If you cry, it's acknowledging danger. If you cry, she will not stop." So instead, I swallowed and steadied my voice, not just to comfort her with a white lie but to truly force myself into believing it.

"It's just hair, Umma," I said. "It will grow back."

# 8

# Unni

Three weeks passed and my mother began to turn a corner, regaining her strength by the end of June, just in time for her second treatment.

There was a plan in place for three Korean women to join us, a sort of all-hands-on-deck strategy. Friends and family and hospital workers had all insisted that we would be better caretakers if we also made time for ourselves. With a rotating cast we'd have some breathing room and extra help to focus on her diet, insight into dishes that might entice her, Korean food she could stomach through the nausea.

Kye would arrive first. Then, three weeks later, LA Kim would relieve her, and three weeks after that, there was some thought that Nami would come, but since Nami Emo had been Eunmi's sole caretaker for two years before she died, we hoped it wouldn't come to that, that we could manage well enough on our own and spare her the sight of a second sister going through it all over again.

WHEN KYE ARRIVED, it seemed like everything was going to get better. She exuded calm and focus, like a stern nurse. Short, with a sturdy build and a wide face, she was several years older than my mother, I guessed in her mid-sixties. She wore her long salt-and-pepper hair up in a bun like a proper madam. When she smiled, her lips stretched out flat and stopped before curving upward, as if paused midway through.

The three of us crowded around her at the kitchen table. Kye had come with goals and distractions, a printed packet of research, Korean face masks, nail polish, and packets of seeds. My mother was wearing pajamas and wrapped in a robe. Her hair was patchy, like an unloved doll.

"Tomorrow morning I want us all to plant this one," Kye said.

She held up three thin packets. Seeds of red leaf lettuce, which we used for ssam, a cherry tomato plant, and Korean green peppers. Once, when I was a kid, I had impressed my mother, intuitively dipping a whole raw pepper into ssamjang paste at a barbecue restaurant in Seoul. The bitterness and spice of the vegetable perfectly married with the savory, salty taste of the sauce, itself made from fermented peppers and soybeans. It was a poetic combination, to reunite something in its raw form with its twice-dead cousin. "This is a very old taste," my mother had said.

"Every morning we can take a walk around the house," Kye continued. "And then we can water our plants and watch them grow."

Kye was sage and inspirational and it reinvigorated the hope in me that had been shaken. With my father beginning to flounder, her presence came as a relief. She asserted firmly, "I'm here." With Kye, my mother could really beat this, she could heal.

"Thank you so much for coming, Kye unni," my mother said.

She reached her hand across the dining room table and placed it on top of Kye's. *Unni* is how Korean women refer to their older sisters and close women friends who are older. It translates to "big sister." My mother didn't have many unnis in Eugene. The only time I remembered hearing her say it was in Halmoni's apartment, when she spoke to Nami. It made her seem childlike, and I wondered if in Kye's seniority, a strong new tactic could be mobilized. It'd be easier for her to lean on someone who was older, who shared her culture, who was not the daughter she instinctively sought to protect. Before the strength of an unni, my mother could naturally surrender.

THE NEXT MORNING, we planted Kye's seeds and slowly walked together around the house. My father was at his office and Kye encouraged me to take some time too, insisting she and my mother could manage on their own. I decided to take my first break and headed into town.

For many years I had stubbornly regarded all forms of physical activity as a waste of time, but I found myself strangely compelled then to drive to my parents' gym. Before my mom got sick she was always sharing articles about how often successful people exercised, and I had formed a thought that if I ran five miles every day, I could transform into a person of regimen, a valuable care-taker and perfect cheerleader, the daughter my mother had always wanted me to be.

I spent an hour on the treadmill. In my head I played a game with the numbers. I thought to myself, If I run at eight for another minute, the chemo will work. If I hit five miles in half an hour she'll be cured.

I hadn't run with such conviction since sixth grade, the first day of middle school, when our gym teacher announced we'd have a timed mile around the schoolyard. I thought I had it in the bag. The year before I was the fastest runner in my grade and I was ready to shine, eager to impress my new peers with super speed, only to be confronted by a harsh reality. Overtaken in a matter of seconds, I was a meerkat running in a pack of gazelles.

Such was puberty, one big masochistic joke set in the halfway house of middle school, where kids endure the three most confusing and sensitive years of their lives, where girls who've already sprouted D cups and know about blow jobs sit beside girls in trainers from the Gap who still have crushes on anime characters. A time when anything that is unique about ourselves, anything that makes us depart ever so slightly from the collective, prototypical vision of popular beauty becomes an agonizing pockmark and self-denial the only remedy at hand.

After gym class and when I was still reeling from the shame of my fall from athletic grace, a girl from my class confronted me in the bathroom with what would become a familiar line of questioning.

"Are you Chinese?"

"No."

"Are you Japanese?"

I shook my head.

"Well, what are you, then?"

I wanted to inform her there were more than two countries that made up the Asian continent but I was too confounded to answer. There was something in my face that other people deciphered as a thing displaced from its origin, like I was some kind of alien or exotic fruit. "What are you, then?" was the last thing I wanted to be asked at twelve because it established that I stuck out, that I was unrecognizable, that I didn't belong. Until then, I'd always been proud of being half Korean, but suddenly I feared it'd become my defining feature and so I began to efface it.

I asked my mother to stop packing me lunches so I could tag along with the popular kids and eat at the shops off campus. Once, I was so petrified that a girl would judge what I ordered at a coffee shop that I ordered the exact same thing as her, a plain bagel with cream cheese and a semisweet hot chocolate, blandness incarnate, a combination I never would have chosen myself. I stopped posing with the peace sign in photos, fearing I looked like an Asian tourist. When my peers started dating, I developed a complex that the only reason someone would like me was if they had yellow fever, and if they didn't like me, I tortured myself over whether it was because of the crude jokes boys in my class would make about Asians having sideways pussies and loving you long time.

Worst of all, I pretended not to have a middle name, which was in fact my mother's name, Chongmi. With a name like Michelle Zauner, I was neutral on paper. I thought the omission chic and modern, as if I had shirked a vestigial extremity and spared myself another bout of mortification when people accidentally pronounced it "Chow Mein," but really I had just become embarrassed about being Korean.

"You don't know what it's like to be the only Korean girl at school," I sounded off to my mother, who stared back at me blankly.

"But you're not Korean," she said. "You're American."

WHEN I GOT HOME from the gym, Kye and my mother were eating together at the kitchen table. Kye had cooked the soybeans she'd soaked the night before and blended them with sesame seeds and water to make a cold soy milk broth. She'd boiled somen noodles, rinsed them under the cold tap, and served them in a bowl with julienned cucumber, the milky white broth poured over top.

"What is it?" I asked.

"This one is called kongguksu," Kye said. "You want to try?"

I nodded and sat in my usual seat at the table, across from my mother. I always considered myself well versed in Korean food but I was beginning to question the breadth of my knowledge. I had never heard of kongguksu. My mother had never made it and I'd never seen it at a restaurant. Kye returned with a bowl for me and sat back down next to my mother. I took a bite. It was simple and clean with a nutty aftertaste. The noodles were chewy and the broth was light with small, coarse bits of blended soybean. The perfect dish for summer, and the perfect dish for my mother, who was easily nauseated by the scents and tastes she'd relished before her treatment.

My mother hovered over her big blue ceramic bowl and guided the rest of the thin noodles into her mouth. The patchy parts of her scalp had been shaved clean.

"You shaved your head," I said.

"Yes. Kye unni did it for me," my mother said. "Doesn't it look so much better?"

"It looks so much better."

I felt guilty for not having suggested we shave it earlier, and couldn't help but feel a little left out that they'd done it without me.

"Gungmul masyeo," Kye coaxed. Drink the broth.

My mother obeyed, tipping back the bowl and drinking the liquid. Since she had started chemo, it was the first time I'd seen her consume a dish in its entirety.

In the evening, Kye used our rice cooker to make homemade yaksik. She mixed rice with local honey, soy sauce, and sesame oil, adding pine nuts, pitted jujubes, raisins, and chestnuts. She rolled the mixture out on a cutting board and divided the flattened cake into smaller squares. Fresh out of the rice cooker it was steaming and gooey. The colors were golden and autumnal, the jujubes a rich, dark red, the light-beige chestnuts framed by the bronze, caramelized rice. She brought it to my mother in bed with a mug of barley tea.

At night Kye brought out the Korean face masks she'd left in the freezer and set out a tray of nuts and crackers, cheese and fruit. The three of us laid the cold white sheets onto our faces and let the viscous moisturizer soak into our pores. We took turns with the vape pen my father had gotten at the weed dispensary, puffing from it as if it were Holly Golightly's glamorous cigarette holder.

Then Kye spread magazines out on my mother's duvet and waved her arm over the collection of nail polish she'd brought from home, telling my mother to pick a color for her pedicure. I reproached myself for not thinking of these things sooner. Watching my mother take pleasure in small practices of vanity was soothing, especially after she'd lost her hair. I was grateful Kye was here, someone with the maturity to guide us.

THE NEXT MORNING, Kye was in the kitchen cooking jatjuk, a pine nut porridge my mother used to make for me when I was sick. I remembered her telling me that families make jatjuk for the ill because it's easy to digest and full of nutrients, and that it was a rare treat because pine nuts were so expensive. I recalled its thick, creamy texture and comforting, nutty flavor as I watched the porridge thicken in the pot. Kye stirred slowly with a wooden spoon.

"Can you teach me to make this?" I asked. "My mom said you could help me learn how to cook for her. I want to be able to help so you can make sure you have time to take breaks for yourself too."

"Don't worry about this one," Kye said. "Just let me take care of it and you can help me by cooking dinner for you and your daddy."

I wondered if I should try to explain how important it was to me. That cooking my mother's food had come to represent an absolute role reversal, a role I was meant to fill. That food was an unspoken language between us, that it had come to symbolize our return to each other, our bonding, our common ground. But

I was so grateful for Kye's help that I didn't want to bother her. I chalked these feelings up to the unwarranted self-involvement of an only child and decided if Kye wouldn't teach me, I should commit myself to another role.

So I became the resident recorder. I wrote down all the medications my mother took, the times she took them, and the symptoms she complained of, learning how to combat them with the other drugs we were prescribed. I monitored the consistency and texture of her bowel movements, introducing laxatives when necessary as the doctor had suggested. In a green spiral notebook I kept by the phone in the kitchen, I began to obsessively notate everything she consumed, researching the nutritional value of every ingredient, calculating the calories in every meal, and adding them up at the end of the day to see how far we were from a normal two-thousand-calorie diet.

Two tomatoes made forty calories. With a tablespoon of honey clocking in at sixty-four, I figured we cleared a hundred calories after my mother drank her morning tomato juice.

She didn't like nutritional supplement drinks like Ensure because they were chalky and shakelike, but one of the nurses at the oncology center suggested we try Ensure Clear, which tasted more like juice. These my mother found much more palatable, which was a glorious victory. My father bought cases of every flavor from Costco and piled them up in our garage, where my mother used to keep her cache of white wine. We tried to get her to drink two or three a day, compulsively refilling the wineglass from which she used to drink her chardonnay. That brought us to at least six or seven hundred.

Misutgaru became another staple. A fine, light-brown powder with a subtle, sweet taste we used to eat atop patbingsu in the summer. Once or twice a day I would mix it with water and a little honey. Two tablespoons would edge us close to a thousand.

For meals, Kye would prepare porridge, or nurungji. She'd spread freshly cooked rice in a thin layer on the bottom of a pot, toast it into a crispy sheet, then pour hot water over it and serve it like a watery, savory oatmeal.

For dessert, strawberry Häagen-Dazs provided a momentous win, clocking in at a whopping 240 calories for half a cup.

My mother developed sores on her lips and tongue that made eating nearly impossible. Anything with flavor stung the tiny cuts in her mouth, leaving us with few dietary options that weren't tepid or bland or mostly liquid, making two thousand calories harder than ever to achieve. When her sores got so bad that she couldn't swallow her painkillers, I crushed Vicodin with the back of a spoon and scattered the bright blue crumbs over scoops of ice cream like narcotic sprinkles. Our table, once beautiful and unique, became a battleground of protein powders and glorified gruel; dinnertime, a calculation and an argument to get anything down.

This obsession with my mother's caloric intake killed my own appetite. Since I'd been in Eugene, I'd lost ten pounds. The little flap of belly my mother always pinched at had disappeared and my hair began to fall out in large chunks in the shower from the stress. In a perverse way I was glad for it. My own weight loss made me feel tied to her. I wanted to embody a physical warning—that if she began to disappear, I would disappear too.

THE SEEDS WE PLANTED began to sprout from the soil, effortlessly consuming the July sun with their own undaunted appetites. My mother went for her second chemotherapy. After the catastrophic response to the first treatment, our oncologist scaled back her dosage to nearly half of what we had started with, but the following week was still difficult.

Kye had been with us for two weeks, and my parents began

to rely on her more and more. I started to worry we wouldn't be able to care for my mother without her. My father was spending more time away from the house in town, and my mother naturally found it easier to ask for Kye's help and assistance. I suspected it hurt her pride to rely on me. Even in the throes of chemo, she'd often ask how I was doing, or if my father and I had eaten.

Kye refused to take any breaks, despite our encouragement. She'd spend the whole day with my mother, massaging her feet and doting on her every need, never leaving her side even when I subtly hinted for a moment with my mother alone. It made me feel guilty, even when I was only leaving the house for an hour to run at the gym. The two of them were inseparable, and while I felt indebted to Kye for her support, I was beginning to feel edged out. Even though I had pushed fear of the worst to the furthest corners of my mind and tried to bury it with positive thinking, deep down I knew there was a possibility these could be my last moments with my mother, and I wanted to make sure to cherish our time together while I still could.

When we scheduled an IV drip to bolster her electrolytes, I volunteered to drive her to the appointment. Kye was reluctant to stay behind but I was firm about going with her alone.

"Please, take some time for yourself, Kye. You deserve it."

I hadn't driven my mother since I was fifteen and learning how to drive. Back then she was so nervous, constantly convinced I was veering over the line on her side. The two of us would screech at each other, exacerbating the situation, arguing over trivial things like how soon to utilize the turn signal and which route to take through town.

Now we were quiet. We held hands and it was nice for a moment to finally be alone together. I thought, We could do this without Kye. I could do this all myself.

At the infusion clinic a nurse took us to a private room that was quiet and dimly lit. It was in a building on the University of Oregon campus, across from a sub shop where I used to get soft serve in the summer before heading through a hole in the chain-link fence nearby that led to a section of the Willamette River banked by a rocky plateau. My friends and I used to jump off the slippery, jagged rocks and let the rapids pull our bodies downstream until we drifted a good quarter of a mile. Then we would kick our way to the shore, jump back in, and let it take us again.

I thought back to those easy summers. When my hands were sticky from soft serve topped with candy, the sun beating down on my neck as I unlocked the chain from my clunky Schwinn, eager to submerge in the cold, fresh water that waited. I had no idea what the building across the lot was. A hospital meant something different back then. Had I even known enough to identify it, I would have been incapable of imagining the people inside. What their suffering was like, both for the patients and the people who loved them, what exactly was at stake. There were so many people there with luck far worse than ours, some without families to help them, without insurance, some unable even to take time off while in treatment. Even with three of us there to labor, caretaking often felt like a herculean feat.

On the car ride home I thought better of bringing up my feelings toward Kye. Instead, I scanned through the discs loaded into my mother's CD player. Slot one was my band's first album; slot two belonged to my mom's new favorite singer, "Bruno Mar"; and slot three was the Barbra Streisand album *Higher Ground*. My mother never seemed to listen to much music, but she loved Barbra Streisand, counting *The Way We Were* and *Yentl* as two of her favorite films. I remembered how we used to sing the song "Tell Him" together, and skipped through the album until I found it on track four.

"Remember this?"

I laughed, turning up the volume. It's a duet between Babs and Celine Dion, two powerhouse divas joining together for one epic track. Celine plays the role of a young woman afraid to confess her feelings to the man she loves, and Barbra is her confidant, encouraging her to take the plunge.

"I'm scared, so afraid to show I care . . . Will he think me weak, if I tremble when I speak?" Celine begins.

When I was a kid my mother used to quiver her lower lip for dramatic effect when she sang the word "tremble." We would trade verses in the living room. I was Barbra and she was Celine, the two of us adding interpretive dance and yearning facial expressions to really sell it.

"I've been there, with my heart out in my hand . . ." I'd join in, a trail of chimes punctuating my entrance. "But what you must understand, you can't let the chance to love him pass you by!" I'd exclaim, prancing from side to side, raising my hand to urge my voice upward, showcasing my exaggerated vocal range.

Then, together, we'd join in triumphantly. "Tell him! Tell him that the sun and moon rise in his eyes! Reach out to him!" And we'd ballroom dance in a circle along the carpet, staring into each other's eyes as we crooned along to the chorus.

My mom let out a soft giggle from the passenger seat and we sang quietly the rest of the way home. Driving out past the clearing just as the sun went down, the scalloped clouds flushed with a deep orange that made it look like magma.

BY THE TIME we got back, Kye was manic. She emerged from my parents' bedroom to reveal she'd shaved her head to match my mother's. She tipped a hip to the side, stretching her arms out, and rolled her eyes languidly as she struck a pose in the hall.

"What do you think?"

She batted her eyelashes and pushed her newly shaved head toward my mother, who reached out her hand and ran it along the stubble. I waited for my mother to scold her the way she would have if I had done such a thing, or recoil the way Eunmi had when I brought up the idea three years ago, but instead, she was moved.

"Oh, Unni," she said, tears in her eyes as the two embraced and Kye brought her back to bed.

WHEN HER THREE WEEKS with us elapsed, Kye insisted she stay longer. Why have someone else fly in? She was up to speed and wanted to stay. My mother was relieved and grateful, but both my father and I had started to feel unsettled by her presence.

She was quite unlike the two of us—reserved and precise. She was raised in Ulsan, a city on the southeast coast of Korea, and after leaving the base in Japan, she and her husband, Woody, had spent the past twenty years in Georgia. I assumed that coming from a southern region in Korea and living in the southern part of the United States, she'd have a more forthcoming personality, but Kye was difficult to read. She was unlike most of the Korean women I'd grown up with, who were warm and maternal, referred to by the names of their children. Kye had no children of her own and interacted with my father and me at arm's length. Her icy demeanor froze us over.

Kye had a habit of letting produce rot on the counter. Fruit flies started to gather in the kitchen, and with my mother's immune system in peril, my father and I grew concerned that some of the ingredients Kye was using could spoil. When my father confronted her about some persimmons that had attracted a plume of gnats, she became irritated and mocked him for being overly cautious.

One night, at dinner, I set my place next to my mother's. Kye moved my silverware across the table to take the seat herself. After we had eaten, she handed my mother a lengthy letter, handwritten in Korean, and asked her to read it silently while my father and I were still at the table. It was three pages long, and halfway through my mother began weeping and took her hand.

"Thank you, Unni," she said. Kye smiled back solemnly.

"What does it say?" my father asked.

My mother was silent and continued to read. If it weren't for the drug-induced haze, she'd have picked up on our discomfort, but in her current state, she was blind to our apprehension.

"It's just for us," Kye said.

Why was this woman here? Didn't she miss her husband? Wasn't it odd for a sixty-something-year-old woman to leave her home in Georgia to come live with us for more than a month without any compensation? I wasn't sure if I was on to something or just being paranoid or, worse, jealous that this woman was a better caretaker for my mother than I was. How self-obsessed was I to begrudge a woman who had selflessly volunteered to help?

As her medication took ever greater hold, my mother became drowsy and colorless and it became increasingly difficult to communicate. She began to slip into her native tongue, which made my father especially crazy. She had spoken fluent English for nearly thirty years and it was shocking when she began to forget to translate, to exclude us. At times it even felt like Kye was taking advantage of it, responding back in Korean and ignoring my father's pleas to speak in English.

When we visited with the pain doctor, I caught myself trying to haggle the numbers down, afraid that if they upped her dosage, she'd fade from us even more. Are you sure your breakthrough pain is really a six and not more of a four? With my spiral notebook pressed against my chest, part of me wanted to withhold the tallies I'd recorded, the number of times we'd had to administer liquid hydrocodone on top of her 25 mcg/day Fentanyl patch. It's not as bad as it looks, I wanted to insist. I did not want her to be in pain, but I also did not want to lose her completely.

The doctor could sense my frustration and prescribed a small dosage of Adderall to help counteract the effects of the painkillers. The first time she took it, she was filled with so much energy we had to physically restrain her to keep her from cleaning the house. For a short while it felt like I had my mother back. The next time we were alone together, I took the opportunity to bring up how I was feeling about Kye.

"She does so much for me," my mother said, her voice quivering. "No one has ever done for me what she has. Michelle-ah, she even wipes my ass."

*I* want to wipe your ass, I wanted to say, realizing it was ridiculous.

"Kye had a very hard life," she said. "Kye's father was a playboy. When he left Kye's mother for a new mistress, he made that mistress raise her. Then when he met even another woman, he abandoned both of them. That mistress woman raised Kye her whole life and never told her she wasn't her real mother. But Kye knew, because she heard rumors from all of the peoples around town. So then, when the mistress woman got the cancer, Kye took care of her until she died. Even on her deathbed, she never told Kye she wasn't her real mother, and Kye never told her she already knew.

"And you know she is Woody's second wife, and his children never really accepted her because she was an affair," my mother added. "Even though they've been married for over twenty years now, his children are still cruel to her because of what they feel she did to their mother. She told me one time they made her so upset she had to go to a mental hospital."

THE NEXT MORNING, Kye prepared soft-boiled eggs for breakfast. She cracked open the top of a shell and held out the rest of the egg for my mother to eat with a spoon. The yellow yolk floated atop its silky, translucent membrane. It looked mostly raw.

"Are you sure that's a good idea?" I asked.

I'd always preferred my eggs with a runny yolk, but my mother's illness had made me increasingly paranoid. Food poisoning was no longer a rite of passage. It was a gamble we couldn't afford. Kye ignored me, her gaze focused on cracking the shell of her own egg.

"I'm just worried because her immune system is weak," I added. "I don't want her to get sick."

Kye squinted at me like a smudge on a lens. She let out a soft scoff. "This is how we eat this one in Korea," she said. My mother sat silently beside her like an obedient pet. I waited for her to come to my defense but she was silent, holding her egg in both hands, clouded over.

What a cruel twist of fate, I thought, my face reddening as I fought back the tears. I had spent my adolescence trying to blend in with my peers in suburban America, and had come of age feeling like my belonging was something to prove. Something that was always in the hands of other people to be given and never my own to take, to decide which side I was on, whom I was allowed to align with. I could never be of both worlds, only half in and half out, waiting to be ejected at will by someone with greater claim than me. Someone full. Someone whole. For a long time I had tried to belong in America, wanted and wished for it more than anything, but in that moment all I wanted was to be accepted as a Korean by two people who refused to claim me. You are not one of us, Kye seemed to say. And you will never really understand what it is she needs, no matter how perfect you try to be.

# 9

# Where Are We Going?

"You're going on a journey and you have five animals," Eunmi said.

"A lion.

"A horse.

"A cow.

"A monkey.

"And a lamb."

We were seated outside on a café terrace and she was teaching me a game she'd learned from a coworker. On the journey there were four stops where you had to give up one of the animals; in the end you could only keep one.

It was the first time I'd been in Seoul since Halmoni died. I was nineteen, in between my freshman and sophomore years at Bryn Mawr, and I'd enrolled in a summer language program at Yonsei University. I was staying with Eunmi Emo for six weeks.

I'd never traveled to Korea without my mother. For the first time it was just Eunmi and me in the apartment I'd grown up visiting. Us and the obnoxious white toy poodle she'd adopted and named Leon, because when combined with the family name, Yi Leon sounds like the Korean word for *come here*.

I slept in Nami's old bedroom; by then she had married Emo Boo and they'd moved to another apartment a few blocks away. Seong Young was in San Francisco pursuing a job in graphic design. Halmoni's room remained exactly as it had been, the door kept shut. The once-bustling apartment felt empty at first, but over the course of six weeks transformed into a jubilant bachelor pad. At night Eunmi Emo would phone in orders for Korean fried chicken and a growler of Cass draft beer. We'd sink our teeth into the crackly skin, hot oil gushing triumphantly from its double-fried crust as we broke into the glistening dark meat, and finished with a cold crunch of the pickled cubes of white radish that came with every delivery.

After dinner, we'd tuck our legs under the low table in the living room and Eunmi would help me with my Korean homework. On weekends we would sit in cafés and fancy bakeries on Garosu-gil and people-watch. Young women with perfect blowouts and designer handbags passing arm in arm with equally perfect-looking men, 90 percent of whom all seemed to have the same haircut.

"Which one do you give up first?" Eunmi asked.

"Definitely the lion," I said. "It would eat the other animals."

Eunmi nodded in agreement. She had a baby face, rounder and fuller than her sisters'. She dressed modestly in khaki capris and a thin white cardigan.

It was July, and we'd ordered patbingsu to share to stave off the humidity. This rendition was far more elaborate than the home-spun efforts of my childhood, its base a perfect soft powder of snow slathered in sweet red beans and garnished with pristinely cut strawberries, perfect squares of ripe mango, and little cushions of multicolored rice cakes. A fine web of condensed milk drizzled over the sides, and vanilla soft serve towered high on top.

"And then which one do you get rid of next?" Eunmi asked, neatly skimming her spoon along the shaved ice and sweet red bean, a thin thread of condensed milk trailing after it.

I mulled over the question, envisioning myself on the kind of journey that would involve many modes of transportation. I imagined handling the large animals with difficulty, wrestling with them to cooperate as I boarded a steamer, a train, a ferry. I thought it would be best to discard the large ones first.

"I guess the cow, and then the horse," I said.

Deciding between the lamb and the monkey was more difficult. Both animals were small and easy to manage. The lamb felt the most comforting. I imagined myself nestled in its wool for warmth, alone on a train speeding into the unknown dark. But then the monkey felt the most human, a companion to see me through it all.

"I'd keep . . . the monkey," I decided.

"Interesting," she said. "So, each of the animals symbolizes your priorities in life. What you get rid of first is what you think is least important; what you keep for last is your highest priority. The lion represents pride, which you got rid of first."

"That makes sense," I said. "I was worried it'd eat the other animals, just like pride eats away at your other priorities. Like, you can't really love someone if you have too much pride, or work your way up to a good job if you feel everything is beneath you."

"The cow represents wealth, because you can milk it. The horse represents your career, because you can ride it through. The lamb is love, and the monkey is your baby."

"Which one did you keep?" I asked.

"I picked the horse."

Eunmi was the only one of her sisters to attend college, graduating at the top of her class with a major in English. She landed a job as an interpreter with KLM airlines on rotation between Holland

and Korea, making her a natural translator for my father and me. In the throes of my paranoia at someday being orphaned by a freak accident, I used to beg my parents to write it into their wills that Eunmi become my legal guardian. She was not just my bachelor comrade; she was like a second mother to me.

"Did you tell my mom about the game? What did she pick?" I asked, hoping we'd picked the same thing, that she'd picked me.

"Your mom picked the monkey, of course."

TWO AND A HALF YEARS LATER, my mother called to tell me Eunmi had stage IV colon cancer. She had sold Halmoni's apartment and stored her things in an officetel, a studio apartment with commercial offices on the lower floors. She was moving in with Nami and Emo Boo so they could help her while she went through chemotherapy.

The diagnosis was impossible to wrap my head around. Eunmi was so straitlaced. She was only forty-eight. She'd never smoked a cigarette in her life. She exercised and went to church. Aside from our occasional bachelor chicken night, she hardly ever drank. She'd never been kissed. People like this did not get cancer.

I googled adenomatous polyps, the little mushroom-shaped growths, poisonous mushrooms that had blossomed into large, malignant flowers from the pinkish-brown tissue bed of my aunt's colon. I know now that by then the cancer had invaded her adjacent organs, metastasized to three regional lymph nodes, but in that moment, I did not understand the disease. I did not follow it clinically as I did my mother's, the changing statistics and prognoses. I only knew that she had colon cancer and that she was doing chemo, that she was invested in beating it, and that was enough for me to really believe she would.

Twenty-four chemotherapy treatments later, Eunmi died on

Valentine's Day. A cosmically cruel fate for a woman who'd never known romantic love. Her last words were "Where are we going?"

I FLEW TO SEOUL from Philadelphia to meet my parents for the funeral. It was held over the course of three days in an old-fashioned wooden room with rice-paper sliding doors. Large floral wreaths adorned with banners lined the hallways, and inside, a framed, glossy photograph of Eunmi holding Leon was propped up on a wooden easel above a platform filled with flowers. Nami and my mother wore black hanboks and served a steady stream of guests, offering them snacks and pouring beverages while they paid their respects. It seemed unfair to me that the two of them should have to wait on anyone when their grief was undoubtedly the deepest.

"Nami is much better at this kind of thing," my mother confided in me as we watched her older sister exchange the customary pleasantries with a new circle of visitors. It made me feel close to her, an admission of awkwardness from someone I'd always perceived as the paragon of poise and authority. It shed light on a truth I often found difficult to believe: that she was not always grace personified, that she once possessed the very same tomboyish defiance and restlessness with formality for which she'd often scolded me, and that her time away from Seoul had maybe exacerbated the estrangement she felt from certain traditions, traditions I had never learned.

On the final day, dressed in my own black hanbok and a pair of white cotton gloves, I led the procession to the crematorium. The cold was oppressive. The air felt sharp, as if a frost stung through every pore of my face, and each icy gust made my eyes water. Inside, we waited in an antechamber, then crowded around a glass window. A man in scrubs and a surgical mask stood in front of a counter where the remains arrived on a conveyer belt. The small pile of gray dust was not a consistent powder but more like rubble. I could see pieces of bone, her bone, and suddenly I felt myself losing my balance. My father caught me as I fell back. The man in the surgical mask folded her up in what looked like deli paper, neatly and nonchalantly creasing the edges around the ash as if it were a sandwich, then slipped it inside the urn.

After the funeral, Nami and my mother took me to the office-tel where Eunmi had stored her belongings. There were photos of Seong Young and me on the fridge. With no children of her own, she had left everything to the two of us. My mother and I sifted through her jewelry box. I spotted a simple silver heart-shaped neck-lace on a plain chain and asked if I could keep it. "Actually, I bought this one for Eunmi for her birthday," my mother said. "How about I keep it and once I get home, I'll buy a new one for you, so we can match. When we wear them, we can think of her together."

My father and I took the bus to Incheon Airport while my mother stayed behind, tending to the rest of Eunmi's estate. As we drove away from the city, I found myself looking back at Seoul as if it were a stranger, something else now than the idyllic utopia of my childhood. With Halmoni and Eunmi gone, it felt like it belonged to me a little less.

MY MOTHER CHANGED a lot after Eunmi died. Once an obses-sive, avid collector, she let go of the compulsion and began to take up new hobbies, to spend time with new people. She enrolled in a small art class with a few of her Korean friends. Once a week she would send me photos of whatever she was working on through Kakao messenger. At first they were really bad. One pencil sketch of Julia in which she resembled a stout sausage with extremities was particularly comical, but after a few weeks, she got better. I was thrilled my mother had finally discovered a way to express herself, depicting small objects from her daily life, knickknacks at home, a tassel, a teapot, engrossed in perfecting something so deceptively simple as the shading of an egg. For Christmas, she painted a card for me with pale yellow and lavender flowers, their stems a watery sea green. "This is a special card I made. My first made card to you," she wrote inside.

One of Eunmi's last requests was that my mother start attending church, but she never did. My mom was the only one in her family who didn't practice Christianity. She believed in some higher power but didn't like the cultishness of organized religion, even when it was what knit most of the Korean community in Eugene closely together. "How can you believe in god when something like this happens?" she said.

Her biggest takeaway from Eunmi's death was that you could go through chemotherapy twenty-four times and still die, and that was a trial she was unwilling to endure. When she first received her diagnosis, she committed herself to two treatments, and if they were unsuccessful, she told us she did not want to continue. If it weren't for my father and me, I'm not sure if she would have gone through it at all.

BY THE END OF JULY, my mother was at the tail end of her second chemotherapy. Her side effects had dwindled, and in another two weeks the oncologist would determine whether or not the size of the tumor had shrunk.

It was time for me to return to the East Coast. My band had a tour scheduled for the first week and a half of August, the last shows we planned on playing for a while. Afterward, I would pack up the belongings I'd left behind in Philadelphia and move back to Oregon for good.

My mother reassured me that she wanted me to leave, but as she stood on the front porch with Kye, waving while my father and I pulled away for the airport, I could see she was crying. Part of me wanted to bound out of the car and back to her like something out of a romantic movie, but I knew it wouldn't resolve anything. We just had to hope now, and wait. All I could do was know in my heart that she was happy I had come to her after all.

PHILADELPHIA WAS MUGGY. The air so waterlogged all movement felt like swimming. It was a shock to be around so many people again, having spent the last three months holed up in a house in the woods. I could tell my friends had no idea what to say to me. They gave me looks like they had spent some thought on it, but talked themselves out of whatever they'd come up with. The group I ran with wasn't really like that. We expressed affection by digging into one another's insecurities, and this was uncharted territory for most of us.

Peter was starting a new job in a few weeks, teaching philosophy as an adjunct professor at a small college in the suburbs. I'd encouraged him to apply before my mom got sick, and he was hesitant to take it now because it meant another season of long distance, but I felt it was too important a career opportunity to miss out on. I suggested he at least try it on for a semester and we could reassess over winter break. Eventually, we figured we'd move to Portland when my mom recovered. We could get new jobs there and I could visit her on the weekends.

In the meantime, Peter took a week and a half off work from the restaurant to play bass on tour with Ian, Kevin, and me, since Deven was off touring with another band, getting "Jimmy Fallon big." Our first show was at a small bar in Philadelphia aptly named The Fire, as it was next door to a fire station. From there we made our way down south through Richmond and Atlanta for a few dates in Florida, then snaked west to Birmingham and Nashville. It was sweltering everywhere. Most of the places we played were DIY spots and house shows without windows or air-conditioning. The four of us sweated through our clothes every night, and often the houses we crashed at were so squalid it seemed more hygienic to avoid the shower. The van smelled acrid, of body odor and stale beer. In the face of life and death, the open road—once so full of grit and possibility, the strangers it harbored so creative and generous, the light of the lifestyle—I had once found so glamorous began to dim.

My parents assured me I wasn't missing much at home; she was getting her strength back and all there was to do was wait. Still, I felt guilty. I felt I should be with them in Oregon, not sitting in the back seat of a fifteen-passenger Ford somewhere outside of Fort Lauderdale, eating gas station taquitos. I gazed out at the long stretches of I-95 and I knew this was the last tour I would go on for a long time.

After our show in Nashville, we drove thirteen hours straight to Philly. The next day, I packed up the rest of my belongings. Peter was back behind the bar at the restaurant, making up for the shifts he'd missed on tour when I got the call.

"You should sit down," my father said.

I slunk to the floor of my bedroom between half-packed cardboard boxes. I held my breath.

"It didn't work," he croaked. I could hear him on the other end bursting into sobs, his breath heaving.

"It didn't shrink . . . at all?" I asked.

It felt like he'd pushed the length of his arm down my throat and was gripping my heart in his fist. I had spent so much time fighting back tears, attempting to be a stoic force of positivity so I could delude myself into thinking we were in line for a miracle. How could it all have been for nothing? The black veins, the clumps of hair, the nights in the hospital, my mother's suffering, what had it all been for?

"When they told us . . . We just sat in the car and looked at each other. All we could say was, I guess this is it."

I could tell my father was not ready for my mother to give up on treatment. It felt like he was waiting for me to protest, for the two of us to band together and encourage her to continue. But it was hard not to feel like the chemo had already stolen the last shreds of my mother's dignity, and that if there was more to take, it would find it. Since receiving her diagnosis, she'd trusted us to make many of her decisions for her, to be her advocates, to plead with nurses and doctors, to question medications on her behalf. But I knew because of Eunmi that if two rounds of chemotherapy hadn't made a dent in her cancer, it was her wish to discontinue treatment. It felt like a decision I had to honor.

My mother took the phone from my father. In a voice that was soft but resolute, she told me she wanted us all to take a trip to Korea. Her condition felt stable, and though the doctor had advised them against it, it felt like a time to choose living over dying. She wanted the chance to say goodbye to her country and to her older sister.

"There are small markets in Seoul you haven't been to yet," she said. "I never took you to Gwangjang Market, where ajummas have been there for years and years making bindaetteok and different types of jeon."

I closed my eyes and let my tears flow. I tried to envision us together again in Seoul. I tried to envision the mung bean batter sizzling in grease, meat patties and oysters sopped and dripping with egg, my mother explaining everything I needed to know before it was too late, showing me all the places we'd always assumed we'd have more time to see.

"Then, after one week, Nami will book us a beautiful hotel in Jeju Island. In September, it will be the perfect weather. It will be warm but not too humid. We can relax and look out at the beach together, and you can see the fish markets where they sell all the different seafoods."

Jeju was famous for its haenyo, female divers trained for generations to hold their breath without scuba gear, collecting abalone, sea cucumber, and other underwater delicacies.

"Maybe I can film it all on my camera. I can make a documentary or something. Of our time there," I said. It was my instinct to document. To co-opt something so vulnerable and personal and tragic for a creative artifact. I realized it as soon as I said it out loud and became disgusted with myself. Shame blossomed and thrust me out of the dream she'd painted, and reality came rushing back with nauseating clarity.

"I just. Umma, I just can't believe it . . ."

I tucked my knees to my chest and blubbered loudly, hiccuping rapid, shallow breaths, my face red with agony. I rocked back and forth on the wooden floor of my bedroom, feeling as if my whole being would just give out. For the first time, she didn't scold me. Perhaps because she could no longer fall back on her staple phrase. Because here they were, the tears I'd been saving.

"Gwaenchanh-a, gwaenchanh-a," she said. It's okay, it's okay. Korean words so familiar, the gentle coo I'd heard my whole life that assured me whatever ache was at hand would pass. Even as she was dying, my mother offered me solace, her instinct to nurture overwhelming any personal fear she might have felt but kept expertly hidden. She was the only person in the world who could tell me that things would all work out somehow. The eye of the storm, a calm witness to the wreckage spinning out into its end.

# Living and Dying

My father booked me a flight from Philadelphia to Seoul. I'd meet my parents there and after two weeks in Korea, we'd all fly back to Oregon together. The morning came for Peter to drive me to the airport. It was early and the sun was just beginning to come up, casting a romantic light on our dingy block, empty cartons of Arctic Splash swept into piles of fallen leaves, the Little League field enclosed in its high chain-link fence.

"Maybe we should get married," I said offhandedly. "So my mom can be there."

Peter squinted. He was groggy and focused on traffic. The warm orange light of dawn flitted like an open slat across his eye line. He didn't respond, just reached over to squeeze my hand, which was annoying. Like everyone else, he never knew the right thing to say. His method of consolation was just to lie beside me in silence until my emotions ran their course and quieted down. To his credit, that was all there really was to do anyway.

I slept for most of the eighteen-hour flight, took the bus from

Incheon to Seoul, then a taxi to Nami's apartment. It was dark by the time I got in, a little after nine. The air was cool and the breeze made a pleasing sound, purling through the leaves as I crossed the gated courtyard toward the complex. I buzzed in and took the elevator up. Leon yipped at a distance as I took my shoes off in the entryway.

Nami hugged me and rolled my suitcase into the guest room. She was dressed in a nightgown and looked uneasy. Quickly, she ushered me back to her bedroom. My parents' flight had not gone well. My mother was in Nami's bed, shivering uncontrollably and burning with a fever. My father lay beside her, holding her over the covers. The fever had started before they left, he admitted. Not wanting to cancel the trip, he'd pressed her body to his, willing it to stop, willing his body heat to cure her.

I stood at the foot of the bed watching her teeth chatter and her body shake. Emo Boo was crouched at my mother's side in loose-fitting pajamas, inserting acupuncture needles into the pressure points of her legs.

"We need to get her to the hospital," I said.

Nami was standing in the doorway, arms crossed and brow furrowed, unsure of how to move forward. Seong Young came up behind her, towering over her head by more than a foot. It was remarkable that someone so large could grow from a woman so small. My mom used to say it was the influence of American food. Nami said something in Korean and he translated.

"My mom think . . . if we go to the hospital. Maybe. They will not let her leave."

"The last time we waited to go to the hospital she nearly died," I said. "I really think we need to go."

The room was quiet for a moment and my mom let out a moan. Nami breathed a heavy sigh, then left the room to begin gathering her things. The six of us split into two cars and drove to a hospital just across the Han River. My denial was still in full force. I was convinced that all she needed was another infusion, an IV to stabilize her. I felt we could go on like this for years, just fixing her.

WE HOPED that my mother could recover and fly to Jeju in a week's time. Nami had already booked our flights and reserved the rooms. But her condition continued to worsen. A week passed and she remained bedridden, plagued by horrible fever and shaking throughout the night. We canceled our trip to Jeju. A week later, we had to cancel our return tickets to Eugene.

Again I was my mother's companion through the night. I'd arrive in the evenings around six and stay with her through the morning until my father came at noon. Then I'd take a cab, bleary-eyed, across the Hannam Bridge to Nami's and fall into the guest bed, where I'd try to regain the sleep I'd lost overnight.

In the hospital I woke with her at all hours, her advocate. When she gasped in pain, I would ring the call button, and when the nurses never came fast enough, I'd screech and point to our room from the fluorescent hallways, babbling desperate pleas in convoluted Korean. I exiled the nurse who failed multiple times to find a vein, leaving a smattering of track marks on my mother's arms. I crawled into the hospital bed and held her as we waited for the painkillers to kick in, whispering in the dark, "Any second, any second, just another minute and this will all go away. Gwaenchanh-a, Umma, gwaenchanh-a."

The onslaught of her symptoms was like something out of a disaster movie. As soon as we'd gotten a handle on one, something deadlier would emerge. Her stomach bloated though she hardly ate. Edema plagued her legs and feet. Herpes completely took over her lips and the inside of her cheeks, covering her tongue in raised white blisters. The doctor gave us two different kinds of herbal mouthwash and a cream for her lips, a thick green ointment to help soothe her sores. The two of us kept up with the regimen religiously, hopeful we could remedy at least one of her ailments. Every two hours, I brought a cup for her to spit in and water to rinse, then a tissue to wipe her lips before applying the dark-green goop. She would ask if I thought the sores were getting better, opening her mouth for me to see. Her tongue looked rotten— like a sack of aging meat, as though a spider had cast it in a thick gray web.

"Absolutely," I would say. "It's already so much better than yesterday!"

Because she was hardly able to eat, they hooked her up to a milky bag that supplied most of the nutrients she needed to survive. When she could no longer get up to go to the bathroom, even with assistance, they inserted a catheter, and we began using a bedpan, which fell to me to empty. When she could no longer pass food, the nurses gave her enemas. They dressed her in a large diaper and when it released, liquid gushed from the top and out of the leg holes like soft silt. There was no embarrassment left, just survival, everything action and reaction.

IN THE MORNING, if my mother was still sleeping, I would slip on a pair of hospital sandals and take the elevator downstairs. Outside, I'd wander around the block in search of something to bring back to her, to remind her of where we were.

There was a Paris Baguette nearby, a Korean chain that serves French baked goods with a Korean twist. I'd return with an array of glistening pastries and colorful smoothies, hoping to spark her appetite. Soboro ppang, a soft bun with peanut crumble on top that we'd shared together on visits to Seoul. A red-bean donut, a soft sweet-potato cheesecake. Or steamed corn bought from an ajumma on the street, seated on a square of cardboard. Mom and I picked the stiff kernels off the cob one by one, meticulous as Eunmi, remembering how she used to leave behind a perfect row of clean, square, transparent membranes when she was done. I bought jjajangmyeon from a Korean-Chinese restaurant and rinsed the kimchi with water from the sink in the bathroom so the red pepper wouldn't sting her tongue.

"What do I even have left to look forward to, Michelle?" she said, welling up as she eyed the wilted white cabbage. "I can't even eat kimchi."

"Your hair is really growing back," I said, trying to change the subject. I put my hand on her head and gently ran my palm over the sparse white fuzz. "For someone who's sick you still look very young and beautiful."

"Do I?" she said, feigning modesty.

"It's true," I said. "It almost looks like . . . Are you wearing makeup?"

I had never realized that my mother had her eyebrows tattooed. They looked so natural it was hard to tell. I thought back to her friend Youngsoon, whose brows had been done poorly, the right one permanently quirked.

"I had it done a long time ago," she said dismissively. She shifted in her hospital cot, pushing out her legs and shimmying her back up the pillow. "You know your dad should really be the one that's here."

"I like being here."

"Yes, but he's my husband," she said. "Even when he's here he doesn't know how to take care of me at all. When I ask him to do the mouthwash he just hands it to me; he doesn't even give me a cup."

I leaned back on the guest bench and stared at my feet, slowly clapping my left hospital sandal back and forth against my bare heel. A couple years before this we were at an Olive Garden when she alluded to an argument they'd had, the subject of which she'd said she could never reveal. That it would ruin the way I saw my father, like a broken plate you've glued back together and have to keep using, but all you can see is the crack.

"Do you think he'll get married again?"

"I think he will. Probably," she said. She looked like she didn't mind it, that it was something they'd discussed together before. "He'll probably marry another Asian woman." I cringed, particularly distressed at the thought of it being another Asian woman. It was mortifying to imagine what people might think, that he could just replace her, that he had yellow fever. It cheapened their bond. It cheapened us.

"I don't think I could stand it," I said. "I don't think I could accept it. It's disgusting."

There was a dangerous and unspoken prospect looming, that without my mother to bond us, my father and I would drift apart. I was not essential to him in the way I knew I was to my mother, and I could see that in the aftermath, there would be a struggle to coexist. That there was a good chance we would come unmoored, that our family would dissolve entirely. I waited for my mother to scold me, to assert that he was my father, my blood. That I was selfish and spoiled for thinking that way about the man who had provided for us. Instead she rested her hand on my back, resigned to the fact that she could not help what she knew was left unsaid.

"You'll do whatever you have to do."

TWO AND A HALF WEEKS into our disastrous vacation I arrived at the hospital to find my father yelling at Seong Young and one of the nurses in the hallway, the whole hospital wing gaping at the large American man and his large American temper.

"That's my wife!" he shouted. "Speak English!"

"What happened?" I asked.

My father was accusing Seong Young of withholding translations in an effort to spare him from the worst of the news. Seong Young was quiet and nodded his head. He held his hands behind his back as if he were about to bow and listened intently, letting my father get his anger out. The nurse looked nervous and desperate to back away. Inside, my mother was unconscious, her mouth covered by an oxygen mask hooked up to what looked like a high-tech vacuum. Nami was standing over her bed, a taut fist held to her lips. She must have known all along that this was what we were in for.

Seong Young and my father returned, our pretty young doctor filing in behind them. I was shocked by the amount of time the doctor spent with us in Korea. In Oregon, I couldn't recall seeing a doctor for more than a minute before they rushed off to another room and left the nurses in charge. Here, our doctor seemed genuinely interested in helping us, had even held my mother's hand when we first arrived. Though she seemed to know quite a bit of English, she was always apologizing for her inability to speak it well. She informed us that my mother had gone into septic shock. That her blood pressure was dangerously low and she would likely have to be moved to a ventilator to stay alive.

It used to be so clear to me, the difference between living and dying. My mother and I had always agreed that we'd rather end our lives than live on as vegetables. But now that we had to confront it, the shreds of physical autonomy torn more ragged every day, the divide had blurred. She was bedridden, unable to walk on her own, her bowels no longer moving. She ate through a bag dripped through her arm and now she could no longer breathe without a machine. It was getting harder every day to say that this was really living.

———

I WATCHED the arc of the elevator lights illuminate from five to three as my father and I descended, skipping a nonexistent fourth floor, which is considered bad luck because the pronunciation of the number four in Korean recalls the Chinese character for death. My father and I were silent. We'd decided to go out for some fresh air before confronting the decision of how long we'd keep her intubated if that's what it came to. It was dark out already. Yellow streetlights mobbed by late summer bugs lit the few blocks we walked before we ducked into the nearest bar. We ordered two pints of Kloud and brought them up to the roof, which was empty. We sat at a picnic table and my father reached out for me across the table, closing his large, calloused hand around mine.

"So this is really it," he said.

He squinted at the surface of the picnic table and with his free hand probed a knot in the wood with his index finger. Then he sniffed loudly and wiped the table with his palm, as if dusting it off. He took a sip of his beer and looked back out at the city as if he was searching for its opinion.

"Wow," he said, and let go of my hand.

A cool breeze passed and I felt a chill. I was wearing the same cotton summer dress and hospital slides I'd worn practically every day since we'd gotten here. I could hear the whir of a bike engine passing on the street below and remembered how when I was five or so my father used to take me out on his motorcycle. He'd prop me up in front between his legs, and I'd hang on to the gas cap for support. On long drives the rumble of the engine and the warmth of the gas tank below would put me to sleep, and sometimes when I'd wake up we'd already be back in our driveway. And I wished I could go back there then, back before I knew of a single bad thing.

We had gone out on a limb, traveling to Korea against the doctor's orders. We had tried to plan something that was worth fighting for, and yet every day had wound up worse than the last. We had tried to choose living over dying and it had turned out to be a horrible mistake. We drank another round, tried to let it wash us over.

WE COULDN'T HAVE BEEN GONE more than two hours, but when we returned my mother was sitting upright. Her eyes were wide and alert, like a bewildered child who has just walked into a room and interrupted a tense discussion between adults.

"Did you guys get something to eat?" she asked.

We took it as a sign. My father began to make arrangements for a medical evacuation back to Oregon. We would have to fly with a registered nurse, and once we arrived in Eugene, immediately check back in to Riverbend. I left the room to phone Peter, hoping to return with something to look forward to.

I walked down the hall and slipped out onto the fire escape, a concrete landing enclosed by tan metal bars. I sat and rested my feet on a step. Peter was on vacation with his family for the weekend in Martha's Vineyard, where it was early morning.

"We have to get married," I said.

Honestly, I'd never thought too much about getting married. Since I was a teenager I'd always enjoyed dating and being in love, but most of my thoughts about the future revolved around making it in a rock band. That fantasy alone kept me occupied for a good ten years. I didn't know the names of necklines or silhouettes, species of flowers or cuts of diamonds. In no corner of my mind was there even a vague notion of how I'd like to wear my hair or what color the linens might be. What I did know for certain was that my mom had opinions enough for both of us. In fact, the only thing I'd always known was that if I ever did get married, my mother would be the one who made sure it was perfect. If she wasn't there, I was guaranteed to spend the day wondering what she would've thought. If the table settings looked cheap, if the flower arrangements were middling, if my makeup was too heavy or my dress unflattering. It'd be impossible to feel beautiful without her approval. If she wasn't there, I knew I was destined to be a joyless bride.

"If this is something you could see yourself doing in five years and we don't just do it now, I don't think I will be able to forgive you," I said.

There was a pregnant pause on the other end of the line, and it occurred to me I had no idea where Martha's Vineyard even was. At the time I thought his family was visiting the dusty groves of an actual vineyard. It was one of those novel differences between East and West Coasters that charmed me every so often, like when he referred to the coast as the shore or his indifference to the appearance of fireflies.

"Okay."

"Okay?" I repeated.

"Okay, yeah!" he said. "Let's do it."

I bounded down the sterile, fluorescent hallway, my chest thumping as I passed the dark, curtained-off quarters of other patients, their heart monitors blinking, green lines zigzagging up and down. I returned to my mother's room and told her she had to get better. She had to get home to Eugene and watch her only daughter get married.

THE NEXT DAY I looked up wedding planners online. Pacing outside my mother's hospital room, I explained our situation and found one who was willing to make it work in three weeks' time. Within the hour she emailed me a checklist of things to go over.

Seong Young took me to try on wedding dresses. I sent my mother photos of the different bodices and skirts over Kakao. We decided on a four-hundred-dollar strapless dress with a simple ankle-length tulle skirt. The tailor took my measurements and two days later they delivered it to my mother's hospital room, where I modeled it for her in person.

I knew Nami and Seong Young thought I was crazy. What if she died the day before the wedding? Or was too sick to stand up? I knew it was risky to add even more pressure to already tumultuous circumstances, and yet it felt like the perfect way to shed light on the darkest of situations. Instead of mulling over blood thinners and Fentanyl, we could discuss Chiavari chairs and macarons and dress shoes. Instead of bedsores and catheters, it'd be color schemes and updos and shrimp cocktail. Something to fight for, a celebration to look forward to.

Six days later, my mother was finally released. As we wheeled her toward the elevator our doctor stopped us in the hall to give her a parting gift. "I saw this and thought of you," she said, taking my mother's hand. It was a small hand-carved wooden statue of a family—a father, mother, and daughter holding one another. They were faceless, huddled close, connected as if whittled from the same piece of wood.

# What Procellous Awesomeness Does Not in You Abound?

I met Peter when I was twenty-three. One night in February, Deven invited us all out to a bar after band practice. His childhood friend had just moved back to town after grad school in New York and was celebrating his twenty-fifth birthday at 12 Steps Down, a smoking bar in South Philly where you literally had to descend twelve steps to enter. At the time, we were a band of smokers and it was incentive enough to be able to smoke inside during the dead of winter. We all lit up before we'd even had the chance to order a beer.

It was karaoke night and Peter was up to sing as we filtered in. He'd picked a Billy Joel song called "Scenes from an Italian Restaurant." I'd never heard the song, but I was impressed that among all the other hipsters who'd signed up for Weezer and Blink 182 standards, this guy decided to take on a mom-rock track with a forty-eight-bar instrumental break. He was wearing aviator eyeglasses with thin wire frames that took up practically half his face and a white T-shirt that plunged comically in a deep V, exposing an expansive tuft of curly brown plumage. He held the microphone as if it were the stem of a wineglass—daintily by his fingertips—and proceeded to move along bizarrely to the song, bobbing his head up and down atilt like it'd been partially lopped off and left to flap on a hinge, and tapping his corresponding foot on every quarter note like Mick Jagger at a square dance.

Having sung for a full six and a half minutes and sufficiently aroused the collective indignation of the karaoke waiting list that made up half the bar, Peter embraced Deven, who quipped something inaudible over the music. What I could hear was Peter's laugh, a high-pitched, honking sound that was like a cross between a Muppet and a five-year-old girl. And that was it—I was in love.

It took Peter much longer to discover reciprocal feelings—or perhaps more accurately, for me to implant them. He was out of my league, objectively more attractive, his handsomeness even becoming a running joke among our dowdy friend group. He was a proficient guitar player but interested in more sophisticated endeavors—compiling redacted poetry, translating three-quarters of a novella. He had a master's degree and was fluent in French and had read all seven volumes of *In Search of Lost Time*.

Still, I was determined and spent the next six months pursuing him, assiduous in my efforts to show up at all the same parties and eventually securing weekly face time when I got him a part-time job as a food runner at the Mexican-fusion restaurant where I worked. But even then, after nearly three months of food service camaraderie—cozying up at the service station with the crossword, polishing glasses and folding linens side by side, rushing after cash-outs to make last call—I remained deep in the friend zone.

By October we were gearing up for Restaurant Week, the busiest time of the year. Every fall a slew of suburban families pours into "upscale" Mexican restaurants like ours to dine on three courses for thirty-three bucks, while the chefs sweat and curse, pounding out ceviche after haphazard ceviche and hundreds of deconstructed tamales and miniature tres leches, struggling to fill what feels like a never-ending trough to feed the frugal hordes. That year Restaurant Week became Restaurant *Weeks,* much to the delight of participating restaurant owners eager to cash in, and equally to the chagrin of severely understaffed staffs such as ours, who were expected to work triple the headcount without a single day off.

Peter and I were scheduled to work the night of the kickoff together. I arrived at three thirty to set up for the night and was surprised to find Adam, our bald aggro manager, who frequently threatened to fine us for every glassware casualty, sitting unusually still at the bar, staring into his phone.

"Peter's been in an accident," he said.

An accident was an odd way to refer to it, though in the months that followed, I'd often find myself referring to it that way as well, as if subconsciously we didn't want to acknowledge it for what it was. Peter had been attacked. Adam stood and showed me the photo. He was sitting upright in a hospital bed, his paper gown open in the front, a number of sticky circles adhered to his chest. His face was unrecognizably deformed, the upper left quadrant purple and lopsided.

The night before, Peter and his friend Sean had been walking home late from a party. They turned down the alley that led to Peter's apartment and as they reached the front door someone called out from behind, asking to bum a cigarette. When they turned their heads to oblige, his accomplice swung a brick, knocking them both unconscious. By the time they came to, the attackers had fled. Sean's teeth were missing and he began searching for them in the dark alley. Peter's orbital bone, the socket that houses the eye, was crushed. Nothing had even been stolen. Peter's roommate found them bloodied on the stairwell and took them to the hospital. They were keeping him at Hahnemann for a few days to monitor the bleeding in his brain from the impact.

That night, as I ran up and down serving both floors of the restaurant alone, I couldn't stop thinking about Peter. What could have happened if that brick had been swung with a flick more force, if the bone had traveled half a fingernail further into his brain. And the more I thought about it, the more I realized how much I really did love him. The next morning, I stuffed my backpack full of the most impressive books on my shelf, bought a bouquet of sunflowers and two miniature pumpkins, and rode my bike to the hospital.

Peter was there with his parents, whom I'd met once before at the restaurant. He looked even worse in person, groggy and full of drugs, but I was relieved that he still managed to laugh when the nurse brought out a catheter drainage bottle to hold my flowers.

When he got out of the hospital, Peter went back to his parents' house in Bucks County for a few weeks to recover. When he finally came back to work, I figured things would be different, that he might be rattled and skittish, afraid to walk alone at night. I couldn't imagine he'd want to come out to the bars with us after work. But it seemed that the only thing that had really changed about him were his feelings for me. From then on, the running joke was that I'd paid the two guys to knock some sense into him.

THE PROSPECT of the wedding worked its magic. With the exception of a minor feud with TSA over a heating pad, my mother's medical evacuation went smoothly. The insurance company paid for us to fly business-class and our registered nurse even turned a blind eye to let my mom have a couple of sips of champagne to celebrate. After another week of recovery at Riverbend, my mother was finally able to return home.

It felt like we'd thrown open a shade and the room was filled with new light. My mother had something to fight for, and we used her desire as leverage to get her to move and eat. Suddenly she was in her reading glasses, scrolling through her phone, searching for an engagement ring she remembered seeing at Costco. She held up the screen for me to see. A simple silver band of small diamonds. "Tell Peter to buy you this one," she said.

I sent Peter the link. On the phone we arranged travel plans around his work schedule. He'd fly in one weekend to propose and visit the rental outlet the wedding planner had suggested. Two weeks later he'd return with his family for the real thing.

"We can always get divorced if things go sour," I said to him on the phone. "We can be, like, hip young divorced people."

"We're not going to get a divorce," Peter said.

"I know but if we did, don't you think 'my first husband' would make me sound so full of maturity and mystique?"

WHEN THE TIME CAME I picked him up from the Portland airport. It'd been nearly a month since we'd seen each other, and even though I had basically forced him to propose and even picked the ring, I felt giddy around him in a new way. We drove into the city and parked the car. On the walk to a restaurant, on a random street in the Pearl District, he got down on one knee.

The next day the two of us drove to the wedding outlet and took photos of various chairs and linens to send to my mother. We figured the easiest and most affordable option was to throw a small wedding in my parents' backyard. We had space for a hundred people, and if my mother felt unwell, she could retire to her bedroom without difficulty.

Back on the East Coast, Peter drafted invitations and sent them out express. He made up place cards with all the guests' names and imagined heraldic mottoes to add his own touch. "Kunst, Macht, Kunst," "Art, Power, Art," read one, below an emblem he'd made

with our initials that resembled a coat of arms. "Cervus Non Ser-
vus," "The Stag Is Not Enslaved," read another.

I ordered the cake at a grocery store, bringing back samples first
for my mother to try. I asked my friends in And And And if they'd
be the house band and found a bartender, a photographer, an offi-
ciant. My mother and I lay in bed together and discussed the guest
list and arranged the seating chart. I thought of how we could have
run circles around our wedding planner if only my mom had been
in the right state of mind, if we had the time, if she wasn't squinting to see through the occlusions of OxyContin and Fentanyl.

THERE WERE OTHER MATTERS to attend to that weren't so pleasant. My father scheduled a meeting with hospice. Assisted suicide
was a legal option in Oregon, but the doctor insisted it was his job
to ensure she wasn't in any pain.

As soon as Peter left, Kye returned from Georgia and lobbied
a group of Korean church women to gather in my mother's bedroom and have her properly convert to Christianity. I peered shyly
through the bedroom door. They were singing Korean hymns and
fanning their Bibles while my mother vaguely participated, nodding in and out.

I knew my mom appreciated Kye's generosity and was giving in
to the charade to make her happy, but I'd always been proud of her
resistance to spiritual conformity and I was sorry to see it surrendered. My mother had never practiced religion, even when it separated her from an already meager Korean community in a small
town, even when her sister asked her to on her deathbed. I loved
that she did not fear god. I loved that she believed in reincarnation,
the idea that after all this she could start anew. When I asked her
what she'd want to come back as, she always told me she'd like to
return as a tree. It was a strange and comforting answer, that rather

than something grand and heroic, my mother preferred to return to life as something humble and still.

"Did you accept Jesus into your heart?" I asked.

"Ya, I guess so," she said.

I CROSSED THE ROOM and made my way toward her bedside, but before I crawled in beside her, she asked me to bring her jewelry box. It was a small cherrywood chest with two drawers that slid open from the bottom and a compartment with a mirror that opened from the top. Inside it was lined in dark blue velvet, each drawer divided into nine compartments. None of the jewelry was particularly old. My mother hadn't inherited anything. The pieces were all bought within her lifetime, most of them gifts she'd given herself that were precious to her simply because of her ability to do so.

"I'm going to give away some of my jewelry this week," she said. "But I want you to pick what you want first."

This, more than anything, felt like an expression of my mother's spirituality. For my mother, nothing was holier than a woman's accessories. I traced my fingers over her necklaces and earrings, selfishly wanting to keep it all, even though I knew I'd never wear most of it.

I didn't know anything about jewelry. I didn't know what made one piece more valuable than another, how to distinguish silver from steel or diamond from glass, whether or not a pearl was real or plastic. The pieces that meant the most to me weren't worth much. They were ones that recalled specific memories, more like Monopoly tokens than precious gems. A small pendant in the shape of a stick figure with my birthstone stuck in its belly, its arms and legs fake gold chains that hung from its sides. A cheap glass beaded bracelet she bought from a beach peddler on a vacation in Mexico. The Scottie dog brooch that was pinned to her lapel while we waited on the couch for Dad to finish in the bathroom and drive us to Uncle Ron's for Thanksgiving. A gaudy butterfly ring I teased her about over a holiday dinner. Most important, Eunmi's necklace that matched my own.

EVERY DAY leading up to the wedding, my mother and I would walk the circumference of the house. She'd set a goal to slow dance with her son-in-law and we were working on building up her stamina. It was late September and the pine needles were beginning to yellow and fall, the mornings becoming brisker. Arm in arm, we'd start from the sliding door off the living room and walk down the three wooden steps of the deck, pacing slowly across the lawn, hugging the bark mulch past the rhododendrons my mother had planted years before. Julia would follow close behind, desperate for my mother's affection, which we had nervously discouraged for fear of germs. Occasionally she would stop to pull a weed before we rounded the concrete drive and retreated, victorious, back inside.

LA Kim flew in a week before the wedding, her hair neatly cropped, nails garishly adorned with many small crystals. She and my mother caught up in her bedroom while Kye presided over them like a disapproving nun. LA Kim was as warm and cheerful as Kye was cold and distant. I had always liked her and I was eager to have another person on my side, a Korean woman who could stand up to Kye and offer perspective. Also, my mother had always complimented her cooking.

LA Kim woke up early the next morning to prepare nurungji for my mother, just as Kye had done. She pressed the rice against the bottom of the pot, browning it to a golden hue, then added hot water to create a light porridge. She snuck in a bit of poached chicken, a little extra protein for my mother's meal.

"Oh, this taste, it's too strong," my mother said.

"Why would you do that?" Kye snapped. She rolled her eyes and took the bowl away.

Booted from the cooking, LA Kim focused her energy elsewhere. She went through the kitchen cabinets, filling garbage bags with the expired cans my mother had accumulated in the pantries, and volunteered to prepare the galbi, my favorite celebratory Korean dish, for our wedding.

Once, when I was in college, my mother walked me through her recipe over the phone. She relayed the ingredients haphazardly, rattling off the brand of mulyeot, or sweet barley malt syrup, and describing the tin of sesame oil she had at home as I darted around H Mart, struggling to keep up. Back at home, I called again to have her walk me through the process, frustrated that her instructions were always so convoluted, even when it came to making rice.

"What do you mean put my hand on top of the rice and add water until it covers it?"

"Put water in until water covers your hand!"

"Covers my hand? Covers my hand until where?"

"Until it covers the top of your hand!"

I held the phone against my shoulder, my left hand submerged under water, laid flat on the surface of the white rice.

"How many cups is that?"

"Honey, I don't know, Mommy doesn't use cup!"

I watched LA Kim intently as she worked through her recipe. Instead of chopping the ingredients, she blitzed Asian pear with garlic and onion in the blender, making a thick marinade for the short rib to lie in. Her recipe relied on fruit as a natural sweetener, whereas my mother always used mulyeot and a can of 7Up. I brought the marinade to my mother to taste. She dipped her index finger into the liquid and licked it. "I think it needs more sesame oil," she said.

PETER AND HIS PARENTS, Fran and Joe, and his younger brother, Steven, arrived two days before the wedding. I was worried they might be upset with me for pressuring their son into a slapdash wedding, but as soon as they walked through the door my concern melted away.

Fran was the ultimate Mommy-Mom, the type that scooped Peter up if he got hurt and told him "That's beautiful!" when he got her a piece of crap for Christmas. She ran a day-care center out of their home when her boys were growing up and dressed as Frumpet the clown for their birthday parties. She made homemade trail mix and something called muddy buddies and chicken stock from scratch and sent you home with leftovers in repurposed cottage cheese containers. She exuded a motherly nurturing that made you feel like you weren't any kind of bother at all.

"How ya doing, hon," she said, enveloping me in a big hug. I could almost feel in the embrace that my concerns had been her concerns, my pain had been her pain.

"It's so nice to meet you, Pran," my mother said, Konglish morphing Fran's *F* into a *P*.

"It's so nice to finally meet you! What a beautiful home!" Fran said. The two of them hugged and it was like Peter and I were watching our worlds collide. We were really getting married.

FLOWERS ARRIVED the next day, for my mother, the most essential piece. There were peach-colored roses and white hydrangeas to decorate the tables, budding lilies, cream and chartreuse, to strew over the wooden arbor we'd pass under in the ceremony. In an old-fashioned wooden milk crate there were boutonnieres for the men, single roses wrapped in soft sagelike leaves, and bouquets bound by light-gray ribbon for me and my bridesmaids.

In the evening a large truck pulled into the driveway and a group of men set up a big white tent on the back lawn, filling it with the tables and chairs we'd chosen. I watched my parents walk out beside it, then stand for a few moments together, looking out beyond the steep hill. The sun was going down and the sky was an orange pink.

They were taking in their property, mulling over the many summers they'd labored on it, the lifetime they'd saved up to reach these years when they were supposed to be able to sit back and begin to really enjoy it together. I remembered watching them from the back seat when I was younger on a drive up to Portland, the two of them holding hands over the center console and just talking about nothing for two hours. I had thought that was what a marriage should be.

My father made no secret of the fact that my parents were rarely intimate. In spite of my secret knowledge, I had always believed that he truly loved her. That life was just like that sometimes.

When my father came back inside, he seemed boyish and giddy.

"What were you talking about?" I asked.

"Your mother just grabbed my penis," he said with a laugh. "She just said I've still got it."

THE MORNING OF THE WEDDING I was restless. By noon my friends arrived and helped me get ready upstairs. Taylor braided my hair into a neat crown and tucked it up loosely. Carly powdered my face. Corey and Nicole, my best friends and bridesmaids, zipped me into my dress.

"I can't believe you're actually getting married," Corey said, gazing at me misty-eyed and in disbelief, as if just the other day we had been twelve, brainstorming names for our tennis balls.

Downstairs, Kye and LA Kim were helping my mother get ready in my parents' bathroom. It felt wrong to be separated, and I was self-conscious without my mother's supervision. When we finished I headed downstairs, anxious for her approval.

She sat on the small wicker couch at the foot of her bed, wearing the vibrant hanbok Nami had sent the week before. Her jeogori was made of bright-red silk, the collar lined in dark blue and gold, with a bright-blue goreum, which Kye had tied in the proper way. The cuffs of the sleeves were white and embroidered with a red flower; the long skirt was honey-cup yellow. She wore a long, dark-brown wig with bangs and a simple low ponytail. She hardly looked sick at all, and it felt nice to pretend just for a moment that she wasn't. Pretend that there was nothing wrong, that it was just a beautiful day for a beautiful wedding.

"What do you think?" I asked nervously, standing before her.

She was silent for a moment, taking me in.

"Beautiful," she beamed at last, tears collecting in her eyes. I kneeled down beside her, laying my arms on her skirt.

"But what about my hair?" I asked, concerned when she offered no feedback.

"It looks very nice."

"What about my makeup? You don't think it's too much? My eyebrows—they're not drawn too heavy?"

"No, I don't think it's too much. Better for pictures."

There was no one in the world that was ever as critical or could make me feel as hideous as my mother, but there was no one, not even Peter, who ever made me feel as beautiful. Deep down I always believed her. That no one would tell me the truth if my hair looked sloppy or if my makeup was overdone. I kept waiting for her to fix what I could not see, but she offered no critique. She just smiled, half in and half out of consciousness, maybe too medicated now to tell the difference. Or maybe deep down she knew what was best, that small criticisms weren't worth it anymore.

ALTOGETHER WE WERE a party of one hundred. One table was filled with my father's office colleagues. One table was for my mother's Korean friends. Another consisted entirely of our friends from Philadelphia. Closest to our makeshift altar, our parents sat with Kye and LA Kim, and my father's sister Gayle and her husband, Dick, who'd flown in from Florida. Across the way was the bridal party, Corey and Nicole and their boyfriends, Peter's brother, and his best friend, Sean. Heidi, my mother's only friend from her lonely years in Germany, flew in from Arizona. Two young Korean women she'd gotten close to over the past few years in art class came with their families, eager to see the friend they hadn't seen in months. My mother had been private about her illness, and so the wedding doubled as a celebration of her life without the added pressure of saying it outright. It worked just as planned, all these people from different stages of her life, all together in one place.

Peter walked down the aisle first with his mother, and I followed behind, arm in arm with my father. I wore simple white heels that sank into the soft sod and struggled to make my way gracefully down the grassy aisle, descending into the mud with every step.

Peter had prepared what looked like ten pages of vows. "I promise to love you perfectly, and this is what I mean by that," he began. He held the microphone the same way he had the night I met him, daintily, with three fingers. It was hard to decipher what he was reading aloud. From what I gathered it was a list of ten commitments, but there were so many words I had never heard before, I couldn't help but let out a laugh when, nearing the end, he intoned "what procellous awesomeness does not in you abound." The guests welcomed the opportunity to release a few laughs as well. When he finished, I read the vows I had written.

"I never thought I was going to get married," I said. "But having witnessed for the past six months what it means to keep the promise to be there for someone in sickness and in health, I find myself here, understanding."

I talked about how love was an action, an instinct, a response roused by unplanned moments and small gestures, an inconvenience in someone else's favor. How I felt it most when he drove up to New York after work at three in the morning just to hold me in a warehouse in Brooklyn after I'd discovered my mother was sick. The many times these months he'd flown three thousand miles whenever I needed him. While he listened patiently through the five calls a day I'd been making since June. And though I wished our marriage could begin under more ideal circumstances, it had been these very trials that had assured me he was everything I needed to brave the future that lay ahead. There wasn't a dry eye left in the tent.

We ate galbi ssam, cured meat, soft cheese, crusty bread, plump shrimp, sour kimchi, and creamy deviled eggs. We drank margaritas and negronis, champagne and red wine and bottled beer, took shots of Crater Lake gin, of whose local provenance my father grew more disproportionately proud with every tipple. Peter and I had our first dance to the Carpenters' "Rainy Days and Mondays," a song the two of us had listened to on repeat on a road trip to Nashville. My father was so nervous about our dance, he cut in fifteen seconds into the song. Peter held my mother's waist, supporting her as they rocked slowly back and forth. He looked handsome in his new suit, and with my mother's left hand on his right shoulder and their free hands together, they almost looked like a couple. I realized Peter would be the last man she would ever approve of.

After the dance, my mother went up to her room. I could see her weeping as she walked away with Kye and my father. I wasn't sure if it was because she was so happy or if she was upset, frustrated she couldn't enjoy the night until its end. I tilted back another flute of champagne. I was so relieved that the wedding had happened, relieved she hadn't relapsed, relieved there was no need to call the whole thing off. I let myself slip away from worry. I took my shoes off and went barefoot in the grass, the bottom four inches of my dress awash with mud. I fed Julia pieces of cake from my hand and sang karaoke with my friends and hung from the rafters of the tent, reveling in the luxury that no one could kick me out of my own wedding. A limousine was supposed to take us to a hotel for the night but got stuck trying to turn around in the gravel driveway, so all ten of us in the wedding party piled in with And And And's trumpet player and rode in the back of their band van into town. Within fifteen minutes of our arrival, hotel guests called the cops and we were forced to relocate, flooding the bars downtown, half of us denied entry, the other half gorging on corn dogs inside, spilling mustard on our suits and dresses. After last call, Peter and I returned to our hotel bed, too drunk to touch each other, and fell asleep side by side as husband and wife.

# 12

# Law and Order

The following days were quiet. It had felt almost as if the wedding would either miraculously cure my mother of her disease or she would just disappear entirely into the air like a balloon. But after the celebration, there we all were again: same illness, same symptoms, same drugs, same quiet house.

My father started planning a trip for us to go wine tasting in Napa, a thinly veiled guise to keep up momentum. If we always had something to look forward to, we could trick this disease. Not now, cancer, there's a wedding! And then a tasting in Napa! Then an anniversary, a birthday. Come back when we're not so busy.

Such diversions began to seem unrealistic. I spent most of my time lying quietly beside my mother just watching television, holding hands. There were no more walks around the house. She had less and less energy and there wasn't much else she could manage. She slept more often, began to talk less. Hospice brought in a hospital bed and placed it in my parents' room, but we never moved her there. It just seemed too sad.

A week after the wedding, Kye finally took a break and borrowed my mother's car to head down to the Highlands and gamble. My father was on his computer in the kitchen. In bed my mother and I were watching *Inside the Actors Studio*. Mariska Hargitay from *Law and Order* was on. James Lipton was asking about her mother's untimely death. The two of us watched as this beautiful, stoic, adult woman immediately began to tear up. Nearly forty years after the fact, the mere mention of her mother still had this kind of effect. I imagined myself years from that moment, confronted by the same emotions. For the rest of my life there would be a splinter in my being, stinging from the moment my mother died until it was buried with me. Tears streamed down my face and when I looked over, my mother was crying too. We held each other, letting ourselves sob deeply onto each other's T-shirts. Neither of us had ever watched *Law and Order* or even knew who this actress was, but it was as if we were watching my future play out, the pain I'd keep with me for a lifetime.

"When you were a child, you always used to cling to me. Everywhere we went," my mother whispered, struggling to get the words out. "And now that you're older, here you are—still clinging to me."

We let ourselves weep fully then, gently clinging to each other the way we had for twenty-five years, our tears seeping into each other's shirts. Over the televised applause I could hear the wheels of a car tread the gravel driveway, followed by the noisy rumble of the garage door, Kye entering the house, car keys flung onto the kitchen counter.

My mother and I let go of each other, wiping our tears as Kye came into the bedroom jubilantly. My father trailed behind her, halting in the doorframe.

"I won a TV!" she said, plopping down onto the bed beside my mother. She had been drinking.

"Kye, maybe you should go to bed," my father said. "You must be tired."

She ignored him, taking my mother's hands in hers and leaning in toward her pillow. All I could see were the tops of their heads, Kye's black and white hairs already an inch long while my mother's bald head was turned away from me, obstructing my view of their faces. She whispered something to Kye in Korean.

"What did she say?" my father asked.

Kye lingered above my mother. I sat upright so I could see the two of them. Kye's expression was frozen in that same flat, unfinished smile. She kept looking down at my mother, who was smiling back at her.

"What did she say?" my father asked again.

Kye closed her eyes and winced with irritation.

"You two are so selfish!" she exploded, storming out of the room. My father followed her to the kitchen. I stayed beside my mother, who was still smiling, her eyes closed in a peaceful haze.

"Don't do this," he said. "She's going to die any day now, and you know it."

I could hear the two of them stomping upstairs to Kye's bedroom, she intent on leaving, my father trying to convince her to stay. I listened quietly to the creaking above as they made their way down the hall, my father's heavy steps pacing, failing to get his way. His voice low and rumbling muffled through the ceiling, hers brittle and unwavering, then my father taking the stairs back down two at a time.

My father returned to the bedroom out of breath, his face cold with panic as if he had just made a terrible mistake. He asked me to go upstairs to speak to her. I went reluctantly, my heart pounding. The last thing I wanted to do was beg her to stay. I wanted her to leave.

When I got to the guest room, her luggage was open on the bed and she was packing her belongings quickly and forcefully.

"Kye, why are you doing this?"

"It's time for me to go," she said. She didn't sound furious, but stern and intractable. She zipped her bag closed, hoisted it off the bed, and carried it down the stairs.

"Please don't leave like this," I said, following behind her. "At least don't leave in anger. Leave tomorrow. My dad will take you to the airport."

"I'm sorry, sweetie. But I have to go now."

She sat outside on the porch bench with her luggage, I assumed to wait for a taxi. It was getting cold out, and I could hear the wind chime jingle from the side of the arbor I'd passed under during the ceremony, and in that moment I wondered what Kye knew about my mother that I didn't. And where a driver would even take her. It was past midnight and she wouldn't be able to fly out to Georgia until morning.

I went back to my parents' room and my father left again to keep trying.

"Mom, Kye is leaving," I said, returning to her bedside. I was afraid she didn't know what was happening, that she'd be upset with us for making Kye angry, that she'd ask me to chase after her and convince her to stay. But instead she just looked up at me with a big dreamy smile.

"I think she had fun," she said.

# 13

# A Heavy Hand

Two days after Kye left, my mother shot upright in pain of a new and terrible order. She hadn't sat up in days, but whatever was breaking through now was something entirely different. Something in her bloated belly must have grown and shifted, pushed up against her organs, and induced a feeling so excruciating it burst through the foamy ceiling of narcotics like a bullet. Her eyes were wide with terror but focused far off, like she couldn't see us. She held her stomach and cried out, "AH PEO! AH PEO!"

*Pain.*

My father and I frantically administered liquid hydrocodone under her tongue. Minutes felt like hours as we held her, reassuring her over and over that it would pass. At last she settled into a deep sleep. Sandwiching her between us, I filled with insurmountable sadness. The doctor had lied to us. He'd told us she wouldn't feel any pain; he'd told us it was his job to make sure of it. He looked into her eyes and made a promise, and he fucking broke it. My mother's last words were *pain.*

We were so terrified of it happening again, we resolved to snow her under completely. Every hour or so we'd slip the plastic dropper between her lips and dispense what seemed like enough opioids to take down a horse. Hospice nurses came twice a day to check in and deliver more medication as needed. They told us we were doing the right thing and left us with pamphlets that listed numbers to call when it happened and what to expect next. There wasn't much for us to do except turn her occasionally, prop her body up with pillows every hour or so to avoid bedsores, pat her lips with a sponge so they wouldn't chap. That was all we had left to offer.

Days passed and my mother never moved. With no control over her body, she kept wetting the bed. Twice a day my father and I would have to change the sheets around her, pulling off her pajama pants and underwear. We thought about moving her to the hospice bed but we just couldn't.

With my mother incapacitated, my father and I found ourselves suddenly compelled to start clearing out the house. We opened drawers we'd never opened, frantically emptying them into black garbage bags. It was as if we were trying to get ahead of the inevitable, as if we knew the process would gain weight and bulk once she was technically dead.

The house was quiet aside from her breathing, a horrible sucking like the last sputtering of a coffeepot. Sometimes it stopped completely and my father and I would go silent for four full seconds, wondering if this was it. Then she would gasp again. The pamphlet hospice left told us the intervals would lengthen over time until eventually her breathing stopped completely.

We were waiting for her to die. The last days excruciatingly drawn out. All this time I had feared a sudden death, but now I wondered how it was even possible that my mother's heart was still beating. It'd been days since she'd eaten or taken water. It destroyed me to think that she could just be starving to death.

My father and I spent most of the time lying in silence with her body between us, watching her chest heave and struggle for breath, counting the seconds between respirations.

"Sometimes I think about holding her nose," he said.

Between sobs he lowered his face to her chest. It was something that should have been shocking to hear, but wasn't. I didn't blame him. We hadn't left the house in days, so afraid of what we might miss. I wondered how he could even sleep at night.

"I know you wish it was me. I wish it was me too."

I put my hand on his back. "No," I said softly, though in my ugliest heart I did.

It was supposed to be him. We had never planned for this circumstance, where she died before he did. My mother and I had even discussed it, whether she'd move to Korea or remarry, whether we'd live together. But I had never spoken with my father about what we would do if she died first because it had seemed so out of the realm of possibility. He was the former addict who shared needles in New Hope at the height of the AIDS crisis, who smoked a pack a day since he was nine, who practically bathed in banned pesticides for years as an exterminator, who drank two bottles of wine every night and drove drunk and had high cholesterol. Not my mother, who could do splits and still got carded at the liquor store.

My mother would have known what to do, and when it was all over, we'd reemerge entwined with each other, closer than ever. But my father was unabashedly panicked, openly scared in a way I wished he would keep from me. He was desperate to escape this excruciating ache by any means, and liable to leave me behind.

WHEN HE LEFT the house to begin making funeral arrangements, I opted to stay home. I was hoping for last words, something else.

Hospice told us it could happen. That the dying can hear us. That there was a possibility she could shoot back into consciousness for one last moment, look me in the eyes, and say something conclusive, a parting word. I needed to be there in case it happened.

"Umma, are you there?" I whispered. "Can you hear me?"

Tears began dribbling down my face and onto her pajamas.

"Umma, please wake up," I yelled, as if trying to wake her. "I'm not ready. Please, Umma. I'm not ready. Umma! Umma!"

I screamed to her in her language, in my mother tongue. My first word. Hoping she'd hear her little girl calling, and like the quintessential mother who's suddenly filled with enough otherworldly strength to lift the car and save her trapped child, she'd come back for me. She'd wake for just a moment. Open her eyes and tell me goodbye. Impart something, anything, to help me move forward, to let me know it'd all work out. Above all, I wanted so desperately for her last words not to be *pain*. Anything, anything at all but that.

*Umma! Umma!*

The same words my mother repeated when her mother died. That Korean sob, guttural and deep and primal. The same sound I'd heard in Korean movies and soap operas, the sound my mother made crying for her mother and sister. A pained vibrato that breaks apart into staccato quarter notes, descending as if it were falling off a series of small ledges.

But her eyes did not open. She didn't move at all. She just continued to breathe, respiration lagging by the hour, the sounds of her inhalations drifting further and further apart.

PETER ARRIVED later that week. I picked him up from the airport and took him to a small sushi place for dinner. The two of us shared a bottle of sake and I broke down again in the restaurant, unable to eat. We returned home at nine and stood in the doorway of my parents' room, where my father lay beside her.

"Mom, Peter is here," I said, for some reason. "I'm going to sleep upstairs. I love you."

We fell asleep in my childhood bed. We still hadn't had sex since we got married and as I drifted off, I wondered how I ever could. I couldn't fathom joy or pleasure or losing myself in a moment ever again. Maybe because it felt wrong, like a betrayal. If I really loved her, I had no right to feel those things again.

I woke to my father's voice calling up to me from the bottom of the stairs.

"Michelle, it happened," he whimpered. "She's gone."

I WENT DOWNSTAIRS and into the room, my heart racing. She looked the same as she had the past few days, supine and still. My father lay on his side of the bed, his back to the door, facing toward her. I walked around and lay down on the other side of her. It was five in the morning and I could hear birds beginning to chirp from the woods outside, the day threatening to begin.

"Let's stay here for thirty minutes before we call anyone," he said.

My mother's body already felt cold and stiff and I wondered how long she had been like this, when my father had noticed. Had he slept at all? Had there been a sound? He was crying now, into her soft gray shirt, shaking the mattress. I could sense Peter lingering in the hall, unsure of what to do with himself.

"You can come in," I said.

Peter squeezed in beside me on the edge of the bed; we were all quiet. I felt bad for him. I'd never seen a dead body before and I wondered if this was his first too. I thought of how cyclical it was to be sandwiched between my new husband and my deceased mother. I imagined our four bodies in aerial view. On the right side, two newlyweds beginning their first chapter, on the left, a widower and a corpse, closing the book on over thirty years of marriage. In a way it already felt like my vantage. Like I was observing all of this and not even really there at all. I wondered how long it was appropriate to lie there, what I was meant to discover in this time. Her body hadn't really been hers for a while now, but the thought of removing it from the house was terrifying.

"Okay," I said eventually, to no one in particular. The three of us sat up slowly and Peter left the room.

"Wait," my father said to me, and I paused beside him as he took my mother's left hand in his and slowly worked off her wedding ring. "Here."

His hand trembled as he pushed it onto my right ring finger. I had forgotten all about this. It felt wrong to remove it from her, though obviously illogical to bury her with it. I held my hand out and examined it. The band was silver and filled with diamond side stones; a jeweled cushion cupped the main diamond set atop. She had picked it herself probably fifteen years into their marriage, to replace the faded gold band and its tiny dot of a diamond that he'd bought her when they were our age.

I was still getting used to the ring on my left hand, not so much to what it symbolized as to its physical occupancy, to the sensation of it. Bound around my finger, it was like adjusting to a brace or some sophisticated article I hadn't quite grown into. With my mother's ring on my right hand I felt like a five-year-old in a full face of makeup. I twisted it back and forth, trying to get comfortable, its facets glistened in the light of breaking dawn, oversized and out of place on my undiscerning finger. It felt heavy. A weight emblematic of loss, a tug I'd notice every time I went to lift my hand.

NOT WANTING to see her taken from the house in pajamas, my father asked me to choose an outfit for her to be cremated in. Alone in her closet I struggled against the hangers, two racks on either side of a small walk-in, encumbered by the weight of my mother's many cardigans and vests, chinos and trousers, trenches, bombers, peacoats, and utility jackets. I picked a simple black skirt with lace detail that fell at the knee, and black leggings to cover legs that had gotten even scrawnier and that I knew she'd want to conceal, though from whom was no real matter. A soft gray knit beanie to cover her head, a loose blouse, and a fitted black blazer.

Rigor mortis made it extremely difficult to dress her. Her arms were so stiff I was afraid of breaking them as I pushed them through the sleeves. Her body was heavy and when I set down her weight, her head plopped onto the pillow and her eyes bounced open. I let out a wail so full of anguish, neither Peter nor my father dared to enter. I kept at it, pushing at her dead limbs, my own body collapsing beside her every other moment to writhe and cry and scream into the mattress. Overwhelmed by wretchedness, I had to pause to let it settle. I was not prepared for this. No one had prepared me for this. Why must I feel it? Why must I have this memory? They were just going to put her in a bag, like trash to be removed. They were just going to burn her.

WHEN IT WAS OVER the three of us waited together at the kitchen table. Three men arrived, covered head to toe in paper scrubs. I tried not to look when they took her from the room but caught a glimpse as they wheeled her out on a gurney, zipped into a black body bag. A half second that still haunts me.

"Why don't you two go out for a little while," my father said.

Where do you go after you witness death, I wondered. Peter backed my mother's car out of the garage and for some reason I directed him to Detering Orchards, a farm on the other side of town where my dad used to take me every October when I was a kid. There were orchards, fields of different varietals. My father and I would spend the day picking apples and when we were finished, we'd return to the marketplace to weigh them and pick three pumpkins to bring home from the patch. One year, when I was seven or so, my dad threw a rotten tomato at me and every year thereafter we'd have a tomato fight at the end.

It was October 18th and that's where I wanted to go. I wonder in retrospect if I was drawn there because it was a place to which my mother was specifically not attached. It was one of the rare places that belonged to my father and me, where if the few trees bore fruit we'd pick an Asian pear for her before heading back. Maybe I wanted to go there because it was a place where I could pretend that my mother was still alive, waiting for me at home.

It was busy when we pulled into the parking lot. Full of families tugging their children along in red wagons while the kids sucked at plastic straws filled with local flavored honey and drank from Dixie cups of cider. The weather was nice and sunny, the chill of fall still at bay. It didn't feel like a day on which someone had died.

I squinted when the light hit my face. It felt like I was on drugs. None of these people could know what had just happened, but still I wondered if they could see it on my face. When I realized they clearly couldn't, it somehow also felt wrong. It felt wrong to talk to anyone, to smile or laugh or eat again knowing that she was dead.

We walked out between stacks of hay bales. Near the front entrance there were Halloween-themed cutouts for photographs and a few lawn games. Further down there was a pen with goats and a little feeder where you could pay a quarter to let the animals eat from your palm. I slipped in some change and held out my hand to collect a small mound of pellets. Peter followed me over to the fence and stood behind me, resting his hands on my shoulders. Two goats rushed over as I extended my arm over the fence. I felt their lips nibbling up the feed, their wet tongues lapping against my mother's wedding band, their gigantic slanted pupils staring out in multiple directions.

# 14

# Lovely

Though my father made most of the funeral arrangements, he left it to me to pick the cemetery, headstone, and epitaph. My mother had made it clear she wanted to be cremated, but beyond that, she never mentioned anything about her service, and of course we'd never dared to ask. I didn't believe in an afterlife, but I couldn't help but want to do right by her, her spirit very much alive in the reproaches I imagined of the outfit I'd dressed her in, of the headstone I'd chosen. I picked what I thought to be the most tasteful, a bronze headstone with ivy embossed along the edges. On it we arranged to record her name, birth and death days, and LOVELY MOTHER, WIFE, AND BEST FRIEND.

*Lovely* was an adjective my mother adored. She'd told me once if pressed to describe me in a single word, *lovely* would be the one she'd choose. She felt it encompassed an ideal beauty and ardor. It felt a fitting epitaph. To be a loving mother was to be known for a service, but to be a lovely mother was to possess a charm all your own.

I chose a cemetery between our house and town, halfway down the hill, enclosed by a long brick wall with an iron gate. My father confessed to a minor fear of burial, convinced the insects would exact karmic retribution for his years spent as an exterminator, but it was important to me that her ashes be buried in the ground. I wanted to be able to bring flowers and have somewhere to put them. I wanted a place where I could fall against the earth, collapse on the ground, and in the various seasons weep in the grass and dirt, not stand upright before display shelves as if I were visiting a bank or a library.

My father bought two plots side by side. He met with a priest to plan a Christian service, which I didn't bother contesting though it felt somewhat disingenuous. I knew it was the easiest thing and would make other people happy, which is ultimately what she would have wanted.

At the blue wraparound desk in my childhood bedroom, where I wrote all my papers in high school, where just two weeks before I'd written my wedding vows, I struggled to write her eulogy, to find the words to encompass her in a single page.

It was difficult to write about someone I felt I knew so well. The words were unwieldy, engorged with pretension. I wanted to uncover something special about her that only I could reveal. That she was so much more than a housewife, than a mother. That she was her own spectacular individual. Perhaps I was still sanctimoniously belittling the two roles she was ultimately most proud of, unable to accept that the same degree of fulfillment may await those who wish to nurture and love as those who seek to earn and create. Her art was the love that beat on in her loved ones, a contribution to the world that could be just as monumental as a song or a book. There could not be one without the other. Maybe I was just terrified that I might be the closest thing she had to leaving a piece of herself behind.

THE DAY BEFORE the funeral, my father picked up Nami and Seong Young at the airport. As they entered the house, Nami moved like a small, turbulent bird, her gestures unstable and chaotic. She released a guttural and wild wail, a sound I had come to know quite well.

I'd never seen her this way. Nami Emo was always so extraordinarily composed. The interior of our house, so thoroughly my mother's and so haunted by her absence, threw her into hysterics. I tried to imagine how she must feel, to be the eldest and have watched her two baby sisters die within a few years of each other of the same disease. It felt like the world had divided into two different types of people, those who had felt pain and those who had yet to. My aunt was one of us. She knew this kind of pain all too well.

Seong Young held his mother up like a pillar. He was stoic, despite the fact that he'd spent a year in this house when he came to the United States to study English. He would have his own grief to confront, but he swallowed it for now. When one person collapses, the other instinctively shoulders their weight.

I DRESSED for the funeral in a black dress my mother had bought me on one of the shopping trips we'd taken to "update my look" and paired it with a black blazer to cover the tattoos she hated. I put on the silver necklace she gave me after Eunmi died and brought the matching one downstairs.

"This . . . Eunmi's . . . Mom me give . . ." I tried my best to explain in Korean.

In desperation I looked to Seong Young for help.

"My mom bought this for me after Eunmi died so we could

have matching ones. But now that she's gone, I want her to have the other one."

Seong Young translated and Nami took the necklace and closed her fingers over it. She lowered her eyes with a wince and held it over her heart.

"Oh, Michelle-ah," she said, putting it on. "Thank you."

THE FUNERAL WAS WEIRD, mostly because I hadn't been to church in over ten years and I didn't realize just how bizarre religious practice can appear to an atheist. An old woman clad in an elaborate robe appeared with a giant rod terminating in a large cross, which she sort of lifted up and down around the pastor as he moved through the liturgy. Then came the Great Prayer of Thanksgiving, which sounded more like a Charlie Brown VHS special than an appropriate reading for a funeral.

I looked over at Nami, whose hands were clasped together. She wept, solemnly nodding along to the words she could not understand but punctually joining in for every "amen." Christianity was a language she understood. Religion was a comfort and in that moment I was grateful it was there for her.

They called on me to read her eulogy. Peter was on standby in case I broke down. My voice shook and I was nervous, but I read through what I had written. It almost frightened me, that I was able to get through the whole thing without collapsing in tears. I hadn't cried much during the funeral at all.

There was a small reception. Cups of pretzels and trail mix had been laid out by someone, and I felt some remorse that I hadn't been more involved in the planning. I felt awkward, like my mother had at Eunmi's funeral, unsure of how to behave. The pressure to perform and cater to others felt like holding in a sneeze.

When it was over I collected all the bouquets, not wanting to leave a single flower behind. I had a selfish, desperate desire for her gravesite to be so packed with blossoms and bulbs that you could see them from the road. I wanted to advertise how deeply loved my mother had been. I wanted every passerby to question if they had a love like that.

We took her remains to the gravesite. The procession was private, just two cars full of the family staying with us. Her plot was under a tree nestled high on the cemetery's sloping hill. I looked down at the headstone.

"Dad, it says 'loving . . .'" I whispered.

"That's bullshit," he said.

AFTER THE FUNERAL, I invited Corey and Nicole along for dinner with my family at a French restaurant that my father complained was overpriced. I ordered the most expensive thing on the menu. A perfect little circle of rare beef tenderloin, glistening with a bone marrow jus, sitting atop a small pool of sunchoke puree. I severed slice after slice of the savory meat, devouring it, piling in spoonfuls of the buttery mash. It felt like I hadn't eaten in years.

As my father paid the bill, I sat quietly, full of food and wine, and finally let all my emotions take me. I had held in so much. I had starved myself, not just of food, but of a reckoning. I had tried to be stoic. I had tried to conceal my tears from my family and at last they were all funneling out. I could feel the entire restaurant staring as I sobbed and shook, but I didn't care. It felt so good to release it.

We stood to make our way to the car and I felt my legs give out beneath me. I let myself fall into the arms of my two best friends as they rushed to support my weight. I cried all the way home, big, comically fat tears, and then I cried hot, small ones alone in my bedroom until I fell asleep.

I WOKE UP in the early morning feeling like my face had absorbed half a swimming pool. My eyes were puffy and swollen. I was exhausted but restless. I thought of Nami and Seong Young sleeping in the guest room two doors over. I envied the two of them together, bound to each other, while my father and I struggled to connect. I wanted to do something for them, to make them feel comfortable as my mother would have. I was the woman of the house now.

I racked my brain for something I could make them for breakfast and landed on doenjang jjigae, the ultimate Korean comfort food. My mother often served it alongside our Korean meals, a rich, hearty stew filled with vegetables and tofu. I had never made the dish myself, but I knew its basic components and what it should taste like. Still in bed, I turned onto my side and googled how to make Korean fermented soybean soup.

The first link led me to a website run by a woman named Maangchi. There was a YouTube player at the top of the page and a recipe on the bottom. The video was shaky and pixelated. A Korean woman who appeared to be about my mother's age stood over the sink of a dimly lit kitchen. She wore a green tank top with a sequin decal around the collar and had her hair up in a loose ponytail, tucked back into a decorative orange-and-yellow handkerchief revealing long, dangly earrings. "It's Koreans' everyday house food. We eat it with other side dishes and rice," she addressed the camera. Her accent was comforting; her words were reassuring. I'd had the right instinct.

I scanned the ingredient list. One medium potato, one cup of chopped zucchini, five cloves of garlic, one green chile pepper, seven dried anchovies with the heads and intestines removed, two and a half cups of water, one stalk of green onion, tofu, five tablespoons of fermented soybean paste, four large shrimp. Nothing too intimidating.

I washed up and went to the laundry room to look inside my mother's kimchi fridge, an appliance specifically designed to keep fermented foods at the ideal temperature. Supposedly, it mimicked the soil of the Korean winter, where women would bury their earthenware jars, storing their kimchi for the spring. Inside there was already a large container of soybean paste. I could get the other ingredients at Sunrise Market.

I slipped on a pair of my mother's sandals and a light jacket and drove into town. The market was opening just as I arrived. I bought the vegetables I needed and a block of firm tofu. I decided to skip the seafood and picked up some marinated short rib instead, remembering that my mother used beef for her recipe.

I drove home and cooked the rice in my mother's Cuckoo. I peeled a potato and chopped it along with a zucchini and onion, minced some garlic and cut the marinated short rib into bite-sized pieces, then rooted around my mother's cabinets to find her ttukbaegi.

Over medium heat, I put the ttukbaegi straight onto the burner, heated some oil, and tossed in the vegetables and meat. I added a spoonful of doenjang paste and gochugaru, then poured water on top. Every few minutes I checked the broth, adding more paste and sesame oil until it tasted as close as I could get to the memory of my mother's stew. Once I was satisfied, I added squares of tofu, heating them through for a minute before finishing it off with finely sliced green onion. I placed little banchan I found in the kimchi fridge on small ceramic plates—sliced baechu kimchi, braised black soybeans, and crisp soybean sprouts marinated with sesame oil, garlic, and scallions. I set the table with spoons and chopsticks, and opened small packages of seaweed, channeling the movements of my mother as I zipped around the kitchen where I had watched her prepare so many of my favorite dishes.

Seong Young and Nami woke at ten, and I scooped up two bowls of fluffy white rice just as they came down the stairs. I ushered them over to the table and placed the jjigae on a hot plate before them.

"You made this one?" Nami said in disbelief.

"I'm not sure if it's any good," I said.

I took a seat beside them at the table and watched them spoon the broth over their rice, breaking up the tofu with the edges of their spoons, steam wisping from their mouths. For a moment I felt useful, happy that after all the years the two of them had looked after me, I could do this one small thing for them.

THAT EVENING my father took Seong Young and Nami back to the airport. Alone in the kitchen, I heard a knock at the front door, but by the time I opened it there was no one there. Left behind on the mat was a small paper shopping bag. Inside, wrapped carefully in tissue, was a jade-colored ceramic teapot, two cranes in flight painted on the side. I recognized it vaguely, a gift someone had given my mother that sat unused on the top shelf of the glassware cabinet. There was also a letter, written in English and printed on two sheets of paper. I put the teapot back in the bag and brought it inside, sat down at the kitchen island, and read.

*To my lovely friend and student, Chongmi.*
*I still hear your laugh surround me when I am sitting and painting in my studio. One day, you walked into my studio for the first day of art class wearing a stylish dress and fancy sunglasses. Then, I thought to myself, Oh, that rich lady is going to stay in the class*

*for about two months at best. However, you surprised me and you never missed a class for a year. I could see that not only were you so engaged in painting, you enjoyed it.*

*You, two ladies, and I had such a great and joyful time when we had a class. It was more like a Middle Age club than an art class. We had many things in common because we were all in the same age group. We drank coffee with a sweet loaf of bread that you always brought to class. We laughed at so many funny stories that we all told.*

*This went on for a year until you called absent to class. You said it was just a digestion problem, not a big deal. I said, "Just take it easy, sister."*

*I still cannot believe that that was the last time you would hold a brush to paint. I prayed for you, keeping your Korean teapot which you had started drawing just before you got sick.*

*I had started to believe in a miracle. I could have returned the teapot to you right after you stopped coming to class, but I thought if I held on to it you would get better and be the happy lady you had always been.*

*The time came where I could not hold on to it anymore. I know that you are no longer suffering from pain, and are at peace in heaven. You are walking to my studio with a bright and cheerful laugh in my imagination when I am in there. But I have to see you are no longer sitting and painting in your favorite spot.*

*Chongmi, you are a beautiful, kind, and favorable lady and I love you so much.*

*From your friend Yunie.*
*November 2014.*

Why hadn't she waited for me to answer the door? Clearly, my mother's art teacher knew she had passed, yet she kept this letter addressed to her. And if it was for my mother, I wondered, why hadn't she written it in Korean? Had she translated it specifically for me? There was a part of me that felt, or maybe hoped, that after my mother died, I had absorbed her in some way, that she was a part of me now. I wondered if her art teacher felt this way, too, that I was the closest she could get to being heard.

I riffled through the bag where my mom kept her art supplies, a canvas tote with a black handle and a pattern of little Eiffel Towers. I thumbed through her sketch pads. In the smaller one were her early drawings. On the second page was the pencil sketch of Julia. The one where she looked like a tubular sausage with a face. I remembered her texting me a photo of it when she first started the classes, how proud of her I'd been, despite the rudimentary likeness, that she was trying something new.

I noted her progress from page to page. The smaller book was filled with pencil drawings of various objects from around the house, artifacts from her world. A pinecone plucked outside on the acreage. A decorative, miniature wooden clog Eunmi sent as a souvenir from her time in the Netherlands working for KLM. One of the short-stemmed glasses with the textured daisy motif from which she drank her white wine. Porcelain ballerinas, one in fifth position, one in third, my accidental maiming left unrendered. One of her Mary Engelbreit teapots that even without color I recognized as the first in her collection, its yellow base and purple paisley lid conjured instantly from the design I knew so well in pencil. On the last pages were three perfectly shaded eggs. I remembered a conversation we had on the phone about them, years before this whole nightmare started, when her main concern had been conquering their curvature.

In the larger sketchbook, the artwork became more impressive as my mother began to work with watercolors. Her use of color was vibrant and beautiful. She'd always been good at making things beautiful. Her subject matter progressed from household objects to more traditional themes like flowers and fruit. She began to sign and date her work, experimenting with different signatures as if each one were its own nom de plume. On a series of three charcoal drawings of bread and lemons done in May and June of 2013, she signed just her first name, Chongmi. In August 2013, on a painting of three green pears scattered flat beside a vase of coral chrysanthemums, she shortened it to Chong. In February 2014, on a pencil drawing of a bunch of bananas, she signed her name in Korean, but added a Z to the end. In March 2014, just two months before she discovered the cancer, on a watercolor of a whole green bell pepper and its halved orange cousin, she signed Chong Z in blue ballpoint pen.

Though I knew my mother had been taking art classes for the past year and I had even seen photos of a few sketches via text, I'd never seen the bulk of her work. The various signatures revealed something so endearingly dilettante. Now that she was gone, I began to study her like a stranger, rooting around her belongings in an attempt to rediscover her, trying to bring her back to life in any way that I could. In my grief I was desperate to construe the slightest thing as a sign.

It was comforting to hold her work in my hands, to envision my mother prior to pain and suffering, relaxing with a paintbrush in hand, surrounded by close friends. I wondered if making art had been therapeutic for her, helped her navigate the existential dread that came with Eunmi's death. I wondered if the late bloom of her creative interests had shed light on my own artistic impulses. If my own creativity had come from her in the first place. If in another life, if circumstances had been different, she might have been an artist, too.

"Isn't it nice how we actually enjoy talking to each other now?" I said to her once on a trip home from college, after the bulk of the damage done in my teenage years had been allayed.

"It is," she said. "You know what I realized? I've just never met someone like you."

*I've just never met someone like you,* as if I were a stranger from another town or an eccentric guest accompanying a mutual friend to a dinner party. It was a strange thought to hear from the mouth of the woman who had birthed and raised me, with whom I shared a home for eighteen years, someone who was half me. My mother had struggled to understand me just as I struggled to understand her. Thrown as we were on opposite sides of a fault line—generational, cultural, linguistic—we wandered lost without a reference point, each of us unintelligible to the other's expectations, until these past few years when we had just begun to unlock the mystery, carve the psychic space to accommodate each other, appreciate the differences between us, linger in our refracted commonalities. Then, what would have been the most fruitful years of understanding were cut violently short, and I was left alone to decipher the secrets of inheritance without its key.

# 15

# My Heart Will Go On

After my mother's funeral it was as if the house transformed and turned against us. What was once a comforting reflection of her individual style was now a symbol of our collective failure. Every piece of furniture and decorative object seemed to mock us. They reminded us of the stories that had flooded in while she was alive—of cancer patients who had survived against all odds. How someone's neighbor had conquered her own death sentence by way of meditation and positive thinking. How so-and-so's cancer had spread to multiple lymph nodes, but through envisioning a new, unblemished bladder, a miracle occurred, and he was now in remission. Anything seemed possible if you just had an optimistic attitude. Maybe we hadn't tried hard enough, hadn't believed enough, hadn't force-fed her enough blue-green algae. Maybe god hated us. There were other families who had fought and won. We had fought and lost—and among all the natural, heartbreaking emotions we had expected to feel, it also felt strangely embarrassing.

I packed her clothing into garbage bags, disposed of half-used

QVC creams, donated the hospice equipment and leftover protein shakes. In the kitchen my father sat slumped over the glass tabletop with a large plastic cup of red wine and called credit card company after credit card company to cancel the cards in her wallet, repeating over and over to each customer service representative that his wife had just died and we'd no longer be needing their services.

Traveling to some far-off place seemed like a good idea at the time. A mental breather from a house that felt like it was suffocating us. So, one morning over breakfast while my father drank his coffee, he searched online for potential places we could vacation. Maybe an island, he suggested, where we could relax and lie on a beach, but the idea of full days staring dumbly at gorgeous water frightened me. It felt too stagnant, too much time to get caught up in dark thought. Europe reminded him too much of vacations they'd taken together. Eventually, we zeroed in on Southeast Asia, a region of the world that had always captivated us. Neither of us had been to Vietnam and it was relatively inexpensive thanks to a strong American dollar. We figured that maybe if we were busy taking in a place neither of us had ever been, we could manage to forget, just for a moment, how much our lives had fallen apart.

We booked the flights two weeks after the funeral. My father wisely reserved separate rooms so we could have our personal space. We stayed in luxurious hotels with rainwater showerheads and grand breakfast buffets. Trays teeming with exotic fruits and imported cheeses, made-to-order omelets, and cookie-cutter versions of local Vietnamese fare. In Hanoi we sat in silence on a boat gliding across Hạ Long Bay. We passed the beautiful limestone islands jutting out from the water, privately weeping without a comforting word to impart to the other. We booked an overnight train north, to Sapa, on a service called Fanxipan, and when we wound up at the wrong station, my father ran around frantically asking the locals, "Where is fancy pants?" while I bought us bánh mì at a cart nearby. We ate the sandwiches in our bunk beds, capping them off with .5 mgs of my father's Xanax, and worked our way through a plastic bag full of glass bottles of 333 beer until we were impaired enough to sleep through the train's violent sways along the track barely two feet wide. In Sapa we rented motorcycles and rode the foggy, winding roads that overlook the terraced rice fields that never seemed to end. But every moment of wonder was quickly followed by a halting sock to the stomach, a constant reminder of why we were there.

Every time a front desk attendant asked if he needed an extra key for his "friend," my father would blush, "No, no, this is my daughter." "This is my dad!" I shrieked at the Hmong guide who took us back for a handful of fried larvae at her home stay. "Then where is Mommy?" she asked as I crunched into a flaky bulb. "She's at home," my father said, tight-lipped and teary-eyed, unsure of how to move forward. This was still when it seemed best to lie and not get into it, when we were still too afraid to say it out loud. "It's just a father-daughter trip," I added.

Most nights, after an early dinner we'd return to our hotel rooms and I'd crumple onto the bed and sleep for fourteen to fifteen hours. Grief, like depression, made it hard to accomplish even the simplest of tasks. The country felt wasted on us. We were numb to all spectacle and feeling, quietly miserable and completely clueless as to how to help each other. By the time we arrived in Huê, we'd reached the halfway point of a two-week trip that was beginning to feel far too ambitious, even painstakingly long. All I wanted to do was go home. I longed to hide in my bedroom and dissociate with the comforts of my PlayStation and its soothing farming simulation games, not wake up at six a.m. to take a van tour of another pagoda and marketplace while my father bartered for half an hour over the equivalent of a couple of USD.

But that day in Huê, things started to look up. We were pleased that the weather was nicer than it'd been in Sapa, that the atmosphere was more tranquil than in Hanoi. The relentless honking of scooter horns we'd become accustomed to as Vietnam's second national language was not as fluently spoken. Life moved at a slower pace.

We shared lunch, bánh khoái—a greasy, crispy, yellow crepe folded over shrimp and bean sprouts—and washed it down with cold Huda beer. We swam in a gigantic, beautiful pool outside our gigantic, beautiful hotel. We watched our boat driver's wife model souvenir T-shirts and proffer snow globes and wooden bottle openers, shaking our heads with guilt as we repeated "No, thank you" to each ware while gliding along the Perfume River.

In the evening we took a cab to Les Jardins de la Carambole, a highly recommended French-Vietnamese fusion restaurant near the Imperial Citadel. The restaurant looked like a large manor out of the French Quarter of New Orleans. The exterior was painted bright yellow. Three large archways, each with its own balcony, ran along the second story, and a porch with tables extended out elegantly from the facade.

We got cocktails to start and decided on a bottle of Bordeaux to share with dinner. We ordered voraciously. The pumpkin soup, the beef in banana leaf, fried spring rolls, crispy squid, a bowl of bún bò huế, and a seafood mango salad recommended by the waitress. Ordering food so as to maximize the quantity of shared dishes and an exuberance for alcohol are the two things my father and I have always counted on for common ground.

"You know," my father said to our waitress as though he were letting her in on a secret. He stabbed his finger in my direction a few times. "She used to do—what you do!"

"Excuse me?"

The waitress was a pretty Vietnamese woman who looked to be about my age. She had long black hair and was wearing a red ao dài, an ankle-length dress with high slits, and loose black pants underneath. She spoke English with a nearly undetectable accent. Whenever her hands were empty she stood with them clasped, one over the other, like a serene buddha.

"My daughter—she used to work as waitress. Many years!" my father said.

From years of communicating with my mother's family, my dad had developed this way of addressing non–English speakers that involves dropping articles and wildly gesticulating as if he were talking to a three-year-old.

"And me," he pointed to himself. "Long time ago." He stretched his arms wide. "Busboy!" Then he slammed his big hand on the table, rattling the cutlery and glasses, and let out a loud laugh.

"Oh!" the waitress said, miraculously unrattled by an American man nearly overturning a table.

"My daughter and I love food," he said. "We are what you call foodies."

I wasn't sure if it was the boat ride we'd just taken or my father's usage of the word *foodies* and the care he took in pronouncing it FOO-DEES that was making me feel queasy, but suddenly the seafood mango salad I had ordered was not so appealing. There are few things I detest more in this world than an adult man proclaiming himself to be a foodie, much less my own father dragging me in to share the title when only moments before he had asked me if I'd ever heard of a ceviche.

"Oh, really?" the waitress said with an enthusiasm that managed to feel genuine. She was really an exceptional waitress. In her shoes I would have pretended to be occupied polishing spoons thirty minutes ago.

I wasn't necessarily proud of my work as a waitress, but I did feel a sense of honor in it. I loved the camaraderie, the shared disdain for the customer—the Groupon users, the picky eaters, the people who asked for steaks well-done and if the fish was "fishy." There was some joy in exchanging your time for cash, blowing it all on the hour before last call, basking in the glory of ordering drinks after serving them all day. The downside was that the experience had metamorphosed me into a neurotic diner. I developed a compulsory need to stack all my dishes neatly after finishing, tip 25 percent even if the service was horrendous, and never, unless it was royally fucked, send a dish back just because it wasn't to my taste. So when my father asked why I hadn't eaten my salad, I would have preferred stuffing it into my napkin rather than cause a fuss.

"I think I'm feeling a little nauseous from the boat," I said. "It's not a big deal."

"Excuse me," my father called to the waitress from across the room. "She doesn't like," my father said, pointing to the seafood salad. He pinched his nose and then wafted the air, pantomiming, I suppose, the smell of a pungent harbor. "It's too fishy."

"No, no, it's fine," I said. "Really, please, it's fine. Jesus Christ, Dad, I told you it was fine."

"Michelle, if you don't like something, you should say so."

The salad was fishy. After all, it was a seafood salad doused in nước mắm, in a country where fish sauce is a staple. But the fact that I wound up not eating it wasn't the waitress's fault. On top of it all, my father had to go and use the dreaded f-word, parading us around as some type of know-it-all food critics and then disparaging the local fare.

"I have no problem returning food on my own," I said, shifting in my seat. "I'm an adult. I don't need someone to put words in my fucking mouth."

"You don't have to say it that way," he said, glancing back at the waitress. "Keep your voice down."

"Would you like me to take it away?" the waitress asked.

"Yes, please," he said. She seemed generally unfazed, but I couldn't help but envision her having to explain to her manager that it wasn't her fault two American "foo-dees" were surprised to find their seafood salad did indeed taste like fish as she reenacted my father's hand gesture. I wondered what the Vietnamese words were for *stupid tourists*.

"Jesus, I can't believe you," I said. "Now she feels really bad. What if she has to pay for it out of her tips or something?"

"I don't appreciate being scolded by my own daughter in front of strangers," he said. He spoke slowly, pacing himself as he stared at his wineglass. He was holding its stem with a fist. "No one speaks to me the way you do."

"This whole trip you've been bartering with everyone. The taxi drivers, the guides—now it just feels like you're trying to get food for free. It's embarrassing."

"Your mother warned me not to let you take advantage of me."

And there it was. He had committed the unspeakable. He'd put words into the mouth of a dead woman and used them against me. I could feel the blood rushing to my face.

"Oh well, there's plenty of things Mom said about you, too, believe me," I said. "There's a lot of things I could say right now that I'm choosing not to."

She didn't even like you, I wanted to say. She compared you to a broken plate. When could my mother have told him this and what could it have possibly been in reference to? The words kept circling my head. Sure, I had taken my upbringing for granted, I had lashed out at the ones who loved me the most, allowed myself to flounder in a depression I perhaps had no real right to. I had been awful then—but now? I had worked so hard the past six months to try to be the perfect daughter, to make up for the trouble I'd caused as a teenager. But the way he said it made it seem like it was the last piece of wisdom she'd imparted before shuffling off the mortal coil: Watch out for that kid; she's out to take advantage of you. Didn't she know I was the one who slept on the hospital couch for three weeks while Dad stayed in a bed at the apartment? Didn't she know I changed the bedpan because he couldn't do it without gagging? Didn't she know I was the one swallowing my feelings while he blubbered on?

"God, you were so difficult," he said. "We always talked about it. How you could treat us so cruelly."

"I wish I never came here!" I said. And because there was nothing left to say, I pushed my chair out and took off before he could stop me.

I could hear my father's frantic call fade from behind as I charged forward, leaving him to hastily pay the bill for our tense, uneaten meal. I turned the corner alone and stormed full speed into the dark. Our proximity to the citadel made it easier to navigate the city. I vaguely remembered which direction we'd come from and was able to follow the Perfume River back toward the hotel. It was a ways away but I wasn't sure I had enough currency to cover a cab ride back.

I figured it was for the best to walk it off anyway, and spent the time plotting a way back to Hanoi on my own. I could take a train and stay in a cheap room and avoid him for the rest of the week instead of flying to Ho Chi Minh City like we'd planned. But then I'd still have to see him on the plane ride back to America. I wondered how much an early flight back to Philadelphia could cost, how much I'd pay to never have to speak to him again.

By the time I'd managed to find my way back to the hotel, my father was already waiting at the top of the wide staircase that led to the hotel lobby. I expected him to look angry—pacing back and forth waiting to really lay into me about walking off like I did, but I was surprised to see how somber he looked. He was leaning his chin on his hand, resting his elbows on the marble railing, and gazing into the humid night with a look that can only belong to someone who is thinking, How did I get here?

I ducked behind a building so he wouldn't see me. I watched him push back his thinning black hair, and instead of feeling angry or victorious, I felt really, really bad. My father had been the last of his brothers to cling to his hair. Now it had thinned to nearly a third of what it had been before my mother got sick. It felt like just another thing he'd been cheated out of, and I got to thinking he really had been cheated his whole life in a way I had never experienced and could maybe never comprehend. Cheated out of a childhood, out of a father, and now he'd been cheated again, robbed of the woman he loved just a few years shy of their final chapter.

Still, I wasn't ready to forgive him, and now that I had my bearings I decided to look for a place to get a drink. I figured I could maybe find some Australians on holiday to buy me a round when I ran out of money, but there were no tourist spots nearby and I was worried I'd get lost if I wandered too far and drank too much. I doubled back to a local bar down the street called Cafe L'ami.

I took a table on the terrace and ordered a beer. About halfway through the bottle a lanky waiter informed me that the music was about to begin and asked if I wanted to come inside. The bar was dark, lit by a purple light and a slowly rotating disco ball. There were small circular café tables decorated with fake plastic roses. It was mostly empty. There were no foreigners, just a group of locals in the back and a couple seated a few tables away.

Onstage was a Casio keyboard, an acoustic guitar, and a small television monitor in the corner hooked up to a laptop. A hostess picked up the microphone and made some sort of announcement. Two young men took the stage. One with glasses got behind the Casio and the other picked up the guitar and began to play. The hostess sang a song in Vietnamese, and I wasn't sure at first if the players were just miming along to a backing track or if it was a preset accompaniment on the keyboard. The hostess was a surprisingly fantastic singer, and the song was a compelling, emotional ballad I wished I knew the name of to look up later.

I ordered another beer and out of nowhere, a young Vietnamese girl took the seat beside me.

"Excuse me. What are you doing here?" she asked. She had a strong accent and it was difficult to understand her, especially over the music. She started laughing. "I'm sorry. I never see tourist here. I come here every day."

When the hostess finished, one of the men from the back of the bar approached the stage, looking back at his friends for encouragement as he took the mic. A waiter came to our table with a ceramic pot and a teacup and placed it in front of my new companion.

"My name is Quing," she said. She poured herself some tea and wrapped both hands around the cup. She placed her elbows on the table and leaned closer to me so I could hear her better. "It means *flower*."

"Michelle," I said. "I'm just on vacation. I'm staying at a hotel nearby."

"Michelle," she repeated. "What does it mean?"

"Oh, it doesn't really mean anything," I said. The man onstage had started to sing and I was struck again by how good his voice sounded. I wondered for a moment if Vietnamese people were born with perfect pitch.

"I come here because I am sad," she said. "I love to sing. I come here every day."

"I'm sad too," I said, my second beer starting to unravel me a bit. "Why are you sad?"

"I want to be singer!" she said. "But my parents think I must go to school. How come you are sad?"

I took a sip of my beer. "My mom died," I said finally. I realized it was maybe the first time I had let the words leave my mouth.

Quing put down her teacup and put her hand on top of mine. "You should sing something."

She leaned in closer and stared into my eyes, like she was certain this would solve all my problems. It was how I'd felt about music once, back before everything happened. A pure, childlike belief that songs could heal. I had believed that with such conviction before I'd confronted a loss so consuming it had rattled my clearest passions, made my ambitions appear frivolous and egomaniacal. I took another swig of beer, pushed out my chair, and made my way to the stage.

"Do you have 'Rainy Days and Mondays'?" I asked the hostess, who typed it into the YouTube search bar, clicked on a MIDI karaoke video, and handed me the mic. Quing stood against the stage and let out a cheer. When the music kicked in she closed her eyes and smiled, swaying side to side.

"Talking to myself and feeling old . . . Sometimes I'd like to quit, nothing ever seems to fit . . ." I began, realizing the microphone was heavily drowned in reverb. I sounded fantastic. There was literally no way you could sound bad with this thing. I closed my eyes, leaning into it, channeling my best Karen Carpenter—that tiny, tragic figure. That starving woman in the yellow dress, slowly crumbling under the pressure to seem happy for the camera, slowly killing herself on live television, striving for perfection.

The bar applauded. Quing took the plastic rose from our table and presented it to me ceremoniously. When it was her turn she of course selected none other than "My Heart Will Go On," an anthem that reigns on as an unstoppable classic in Asia nearly two decades after its release. I thought of my mother's Celine Dion impression, of her quivering lip. The sopping reverb spread Quing's voice across the bar as she belted, "Near! Far! Wherever you are!" and I collected more roses from the surrounding tables and threw them at her feet.

"Quing! That was so great!"

As the other patrons took their turns at the mic, we continued to collect roses from the tables and throw them onto the stage. We danced to all the songs, cheering the loudest when they were through. She told me about famous Vietnamese singers. We talked about our dreams. I finished my last beer and we hugged goodbye, took down each other's emails, and promised to keep in touch, though we never did.

In the morning, my father and I met for breakfast at the hotel buffet. We didn't talk about our fight and continued on with the trip as if it had never happened. We took the train to Hội An and spent two days there. We walked around Old Town, the historic district, taking pictures along the canal. The streets were lined with stalls selling bright, multicolored lanterns and three-dimensional cards. From the famous Japanese covered bridge, we paused to watch the locals push small paper boats lit with candles out onto the water, completely unaware that "Hội An" means *peaceful meeting place*.

# 16

# Jatjuk

We had come to Vietnam in search of healing, to emerge closer to each other in our grief, but we returned just as damaged and separate as ever. After a twenty-hour flight, we got back to the house at eight, and I fell straight to sleep, exhausted from travel and jet lag. Around midnight I woke up to a phone call from my father.

"I got in an accident," he said. He sounded calm. "I'm about half a mile from home. I need you to come get me. Michelle, bring mouthwash."

Panicked, I kept interrupting him with questions, to which he just responded firmly with my name until he hung up. I pulled a coat over my pajamas, searched frantically for my mother's car keys, grabbed a bottle of Listerine from the bathroom cabinet, and started the drive.

By the time I got there, an ambulance had already arrived. From the look of it I was certain my father was dead. The car had rolled and landed on its side between two telephone poles. All the windows were shattered.

I parked my mother's car behind the wreckage and ran toward the scene only to discover him sitting on the edge of the ambulance, breathing in and out as the paramedics instructed. His shirt was off and a large contusion was already forming along his collarbone. Small cuts were scattered over his arms and chest like they'd been struck multiple times with a cheese grater. Police officers crowded around us, everyone just as stunned as I was that he'd survived. It was impossible to pass off the mouthwash inconspicuously.

"I was going to check in on my office," he said. "I must have fallen asleep at the wheel."

My father's office was next to the Highlands, his favorite bar. "They want me to go to the hospital," he said. "But I don't think I need to."

"You're going," I said.

"Michelle, I'm really all right."

"Look at your fucking car," I said, stabbing a finger toward the wreckage. "When I pulled up I figured I was an orphan! We are going."

I followed behind the ambulance to Riverbend, the same hospital where my mother had stayed when the first chemo knocked her off her feet, the same one we returned to after our trip to Korea. Parts of it reminded me of *The Shining*. There was a wooden portico over the front entrance and a stone fireplace in the lobby that gave off the feeling of a haunted lodge. The long width of the building with its yellow light shining out in the night—it was a difficult image to confront again. By the time I found parking and made my way up to the room, there were already two police officers questioning my father.

"Why are you slurring your words?"

"I'm not slawring my . . ." My father paused. "Well now I am because I'm thinking about it," he said with a laugh. The mouthwash was burning a hole in my coat pocket.

"Please," I said. "My mom just died."

I wasn't sure if I was crying out of fear that my father would get a DUI and I'd be stuck in Eugene as his personal chauffeur, or if I was simply overwhelmed by the feeling that fate was out to destroy us.

"I'm just going to go ahead and say you fell asleep at the wheel," the cop said, eyeing my father suspiciously. I felt my dad put a hand on my back to really sell the scene.

We were discharged within a couple of hours and I drove the two of us home. I refused to speak to him. Now that I knew he was okay, fear for his safety subsided and gave way to anger, pulsing through me.

"I'm telling you, I just fell asleep," he repeated.

It was a miracle he hadn't broken any bones, but he was still in a tremendous amount of pain. He was taking prescription drugs, many of them the same ones my mother had taken. They made him even more depressed. He slept most of the day. For three days my father hardly left his room. Part of me wondered if he had run himself off the road on purpose, which only made me more upset. I made little effort to check in on him. I wanted to be selfish. I didn't want to take care of anyone anymore.

Instead, I began to cook. Mostly the kind of food you could crawl into and that required sleeping off. The kind you'd order on death row. I made chicken pot pie from scratch, rolling out buttery, homemade dough, filling it to the brim with thick, rich stock and roasted chicken, peas, and carrots, blanketing it in its flaky top crust. I barbecued steaks and served them with smooth, creamy mashed potatoes or gratin dauphinois or baked potatoes with half-inch pats of butter and heaping scoops of sour cream. I baked giant lasagnas, smothering them with homemade Bolognese and fistfuls of shredded mozzarella.

For Thanksgiving, I spent weeks researching and collecting recipes online. I stuffed and roasted a ten-pound bird from Costco and made cranberry blizzard—ice cream with Cool Whip and cranberry jelly—which Aunt Margo had taught my mother to make. I served sweet potatoes with marshmallows and gravy made from scratch.

Another night I bought lobsters, taking time to observe them in the supermarket tank, sussing out the liveliest of the bunch. I instructed the fishmonger to lift them with his plastic rake and tickle their tails like my father taught me, picking the ones that flipped violently and with gusto. I boiled them in a large pot and set out the same small bowls my mother would for the melted butter. When they were cooked through, my father made two hacks in the center of their claws and large incisions down their backs.

When we ate lobster, my mother used to boil one for each of us and content herself with a side of corn or a baked potato or a small bowl of rice with banchan and a can of saury, an oily fish she braised in soy sauce. But if we were lucky enough to find some, she'd eat the roe, giddily scooping the plump orange eggs onto her plate.

We sat down to eat and twisted the tails to separate them from their bodies. We flipped them over and cracked the shells in half.

"No eggs," he said with a sigh as he continued disembodying the rest of the carcass, sucking the gray goop from inside.

"Me neither," I said, splitting a claw with a nutcracker.

BY CHRISTMAS Peter's classes were finally finished and he moved in with us. The two of us picked out a Christmas tree from the nursery down the road. Without my mother it felt like we were playing house. Peter took my father's role, lying beneath the tree, rotating the screws on the stand as I tried to see it through my mother's eyes and stop him where it looked the fullest. My mother kept our Christmas decorations upstairs in a hallway closet, padded in newspaper and divided into three matching hat boxes. The lights were wrapped around old copies of *Time* magazine that had been rolled into cylinders.

This closet was just one of the many depots my mother counted on to house what had become, over the course of her lifetime in Eugene, an unfathomable quantity of high-quality junk. A decorative wooden birdcage, bowls full of colorful glass cylinders and bulbs, a collection of candles still wrapped in cellophane. Every alcove and cubby was filled to the brim with QVC, dozens of unused eye creams and serums, chopstick holders and napkin rings.

Hadn't Eunmi's death taught her anything? I wondered. Why had she held on to the warranties for every appliance in the house? Routine car maintenance receipts from more than twenty years ago?

In the recess of the hallway closet, I was confronted by the teeming reliquary of my childhood souvenirs. Every single report card I ever received was stored away in a manila envelope. She saved the poster board from my third-grade science fair. There were diaries she forced me to keep when I was learning to write. "Today mommy and I went to the park to feed birds."

I was just beginning to resent her for the hoarding she'd left me to deal with when I found them: two pairs of baby shoes. They were perfectly preserved, one a pair of sandals made of three pinched white leather ribbons that clasped together at the ankle, one a pair of pink canvas slip-on sneakers with a colorful plaid interior. They were so small I could fit them in the palm of my hand. I held one of the sandals and started to cry. I thought of the foresight a mother must have to preserve this kind of thing, the shoes of her baby, for her baby's baby someday. A baby she'd never get to meet.

My mother kept a great many things for my future child. I found it strangely therapeutic to organize them. I spent at least a week sorting my Playmobil collection into complete sets. In my father's largely unused office, I emptied out the mismatched kits and sorted them into piles. I counted out eight teal teacups the size of corn kernels and reunited them with the other elements of the hot dog stand. I found two rings of fire and put them back into the circus. I spread out the articles of the Victorian mansion on the beige carpet and ran my hands over the tiny pieces of plastic, searching for the miniature blue cap that belonged to the blond boy who lived there with the brown-bobbed girl in the pink shirt and white pants.

My mother would have killed me if she saw the things I was getting rid of. School essays and old insurance cards, VHS tapes of my cameo on a children's show in Korea and the cartoons my aunt dubbed. I sold the Beanie Babies we had been duped into buying, the Princess Diana bear still in its plastic case and tag protector. Samantha, the American Girl doll with long brown hair I had begged for, Craigslisted along with the clothes she came with and the extra ones my mother commissioned at a bargain. It was something like being possessed, the rampant disposal akin to a house fire. The taming of this mountain of chattel into a reasonable collection of possessions took on the proportions of penal labor, its completion looming like a deserved exit, a sentence's end.

All these objects seemed orphaned by her loss, or just devolved into objects, matter, impedimenta. What once had a purpose transformed into a blockade. The bowls once reserved for their own specific meals were now just dishes to be sorted, obstacles in my path to leave. The candleholder I used to pretend was a magical urn as a child, a key plot point in my imaginary narratives, now just another thing to throw away.

I filled a roll of contractor bags with her clothing, staging it all upstairs in piles, so my father wouldn't have to confront the weeklong process. One for donations, one for things I might keep, one for things I knew I wanted. With her clothing spread out on the floor, it looked as if multiple versions of her had deflated and disappeared.

I tried on all her coats, beautiful leather jackets, all heartbreakingly an inch too big in the shoulders. I kept the shoes that suited me, though I promptly disposed of her platform sneakers. I lined her handbags up on the table. Soft orange leather, shiny red snakeskin, small precious clutches that hardly had room for a cell phone. A perfect circle of soft black fur with a thin silver clasp and a black satin interior. All of them looked pristine, like they'd never been used. There was one high-quality fake Chanel purse with the classic black quilting and one real one, still in the box.

I invited Nicole and Corey to look over the rest. I brought them into the room and encouraged them to try on a few of her things and take whatever they wanted. It was awkward at first, but after much insisting they finally gave in. Afterward I invited a few of my mother's friends to do the same, then divided the remainder into carloads and made trips to donation centers in town.

I could feel my heart hardening—crusting over, growing a husk, a callus. I deleted the photographs from the hospital of my mother and me in her bed wearing matching pajamas. I deleted the photo she sent me the day she got her hair cut like Mia Farrow, shyly posing as if the hardest part was over. As I organized the cupboards by the kitchen phone, consolidating loose batteries, tossing old photographs of blurry landscapes, setting aside old undeveloped rolls of film, I came across the green spiral notebook where I had logged all her medications and calorie counts. Those desperate sums, that hopeful inventory, recording every coaxed sip and peck in some sad effort to keep pushing through. I ripped the pages and pulled the metal spiral apart, screaming as I shredded my stupid, useless calculations into innumerable pieces.

PERHAPS I WAS HAUNTED by the destruction of so many entries of jatjuk but later I found myself with an inexplicable craving for the porridge. The meal Kye most often prepared for my mother, one of the few things she'd been able to stomach.

I googled to see if Maangchi, whose recipe I'd followed for soybean stew, had one for pine nut porridge. I was doubtful, since it was a far less popular dish than doenjang jjigae, but sure enough, there it was.

The description read: "I can say that pine nut porridge is the queen of all the porridges! . . . It looks soupy, but I recommend spooning it instead of drinking it, because I want you to enjoy the aftertaste. 1 spoon after, pause! And close your eyes just as I did in the video, to savor the taste. oh yummy oh yummy, then start another spoon! lol."

Her writing reminded me of my mother's texts, down to the way she would micromanage every eating experience.

I propped my laptop up on the kitchen counter and started the video. Maangchi was wearing a brown three-quarter-sleeve shirt with a lace decal on the collar. Her black hair was neat and straight, falling below her shoulders. She stood before her cutting board next to a blender. The video was more recent than the last one and the production quality had improved. Her kitchen was different, more modern and brightly lit.

"Hi, everybody!" she chirped. "Today we are going to learn how to make jatjuk!"

The recipe was simple—pine nuts, rice, salt, and water, all ingredients we already had on hand. Per Maangchi's instructions,

I soaked a third of a cup of rice and set it aside for two hours. I measured out two tablespoons of pine nuts and began removing the tips, then tossed the soft, picked kernels into the blender. When the rice was finished soaking, I rinsed it under the faucet and added it to the pine nuts with two cups of water. I closed the lid and ran the blender on high, then emptied the liquid into a small pot on the stove.

"You don't need many ingredients, but as you can see it takes time. That's why jatjuk is very precious. Like, for example, one of your family members is sick, nothing much you can do. When we visit the hospital we usually make this jatjuk because patients can't eat like normal food. Pine nuts has protein and good fat for body so this is perfect food for patients who are recovering from their illness," Maangchi explained.

The mixture was a beautiful milky-white color. On medium heat I stirred it with a wooden spoon. At first, impatient for it to thicken, I was afraid I'd used too much water. Then, as its consistency turned from skim milk to peanut butter, I was afraid I hadn't added enough. I lowered the heat and continued to stir, hoping it would thin as Maangchi's had. When the pot began to sizzle, I took it off the heat and added salt, then poured it into a small bowl.

I cut chonggak kimchi into small disks and ladled some of the brine over the radish pieces. The soup was creamy and nutty, and felt soft and soothing as I swallowed. I ate a few more spoonfuls before crunching into some kimchi to break up the rich flavor with something spicy and tart. That wasn't so hard, I thought to myself, happy to have conquered the dish Kye had mystified.

This was all I wanted, I realized, after so many days of decadent filets and pricey crustaceans, potatoes slathered in the many glorious permutations that ratios of butter, cheese, and cream can take. This plain porridge was the first dish to make me feel full.

Maangchi supplied the secrets to its composition step by step, like a digital guardian I could always turn to, delivering the knowledge that had been withheld from me, that was my birthright. I closed my eyes and spooned the last of the soup into my mouth, picturing the soft mixture coating my mother's blistered tongue, the warm liquid traveling slowly into my stomach as I tried to savor the aftertaste.

# 17

# Little Axe

"We're on our last two slices of the Vegan Spiral," one of the waitresses announced, strutting past the salad prep station that served as a sort of DMZ between front and back of house. She paused to sniff the air and made a face. "Is something burning?"

"Get. The. Fuck. Out. Of. Here!" I snarled, half of my head still in the pizza oven as I scraped at a stubborn pile of burning cheese. Balanced on a step stool, squinting through the gray smoke that billowed from the ripped center of a pie I'd spent the last ten painstaking minutes preparing, I struggled to keep a cool head and work my way out of the weeds. It was my first shift alone in a busy kitchen and I suddenly understood why all the chefs I'd ever worked with hated front of house. It took every part of me not to fling a pizza cutter across the kitchen like a ninja star.

After the holidays, I'd applied for a job as a cook at a hipster pizza shop, lured in by the grit of working the line and not having to deal with customer service. I figured working at a pizza restaurant would be soothing, that I'd pass the hours leisurely listening to

music, massaging soft dough with my fingers—psychically somewhere between the zen of a Ninja Turtle and Julia Roberts in a
Slice of Heaven tee. I figured, like most people, working at a pizza
shop was stoner work, a good way to return home with money in
my pocket in exchange for a little scuff of flour on my cheek.

Sizzle Pie had other plans for me. As if in observance of some
kind of sadistic hazing ritual, the restaurant threw me onto the
weekend night shift to break me in. I started at ten p.m. and
clocked out at six in the morning. At two, when all the bars let
out downtown, a horde of drunken college students flooded in
for slices and the entire shift was a scramble of throwing slice pies
and heaving large, wooden paddles in and out of hot ovens until
four in the morning, when the restaurant finally closed. Two hours
later, having scoured a day's worth of flour from every cranny of
the kitchen, I was finally released to the dawn.

Afterward, Peter would pick me up. On the nights I worked, he
stayed up at home translating documents from French to English,
freelance work he'd found on Craigslist. I'd crawl into the passenger seat, every bone in my body aching, burns all over my arms,
a centimeter of flour adhered to my contact lenses, and between
bites of a leftover pepperoni slice, he'd beg me to quit.

"The money's just not worth it," he said.

It wasn't about the money. I wanted to stay as busy as possible.
I wanted to work my body as hard as it could go so there was no
time to feel sorry for myself, to bind myself to a routine that would
keep me grounded in the last remaining months before Peter and
I left Eugene for good. Maybe I was punishing myself for my failures as a caretaker, or maybe I was just afraid of what would happen if I slowed down.

When I wasn't at work, preparing meals at home, or packing
up the house, I would go to the little cottage at the bottom of
the property to write songs. I wrote about Julia, and how con-

fused she was, sniffing and pacing outside my mother's bedroom, about running on the treadmill and sleeping in hospital beds, about wearing my mother's wedding ring and the isolation of the woods. They were conversations I wanted to have with people but couldn't. They were attempts to unpack the past six months, when everything I'd once thought I knew for certain about my life had been undone.

When they were finished, I asked Nick, who was back and forth between Eugene and Portland, if he'd play some guitar on them. We'd remained good friends after high school and he was enthusiastic about helping me with the album. Nick introduced me to Colin, a pansexual Alaskan transplant with a rifle collection who played drums and had a bedroom studio in town where we could record. With Peter on bass, the four of us recorded a nine-track album in two weeks. I called it *Psychopomp*.

By late February, most of the house had been packed into boxes. March would mark ten months of captivity and it was time to move on with our lives. Peter and I set our sights on New York, where we planned to hunker down with a couple of 9-to-5s and finally commit to the transition to normal adulthood. But before consigning ourselves to limited vacation days in exchange for corporate insurance, we'd have a proper kiss-off. With our wedding money, Peter and I planned a belated honeymoon in Korea. We'd visit Seoul and Busan, and make up for my family's lost trip to Jeju Island before heading back to the East Coast to start the job hunt.

On Kakao, much aided by Google Translate, I tried my best in short English sentences and patchwork Korean to convey to Nami that Peter and I were planning to visit. Nami wrote her replies in Korean and sent them to Seong Young or Esther, Emo Boo's daughter, to translate them into English, copying-and-pasting them back to me, insisting we stay in the guest room at her apartment.

I was hesitant to take her up on the offer. I'd wanted to connect with Nami since she left Eugene, but navigating our language gap was extremely challenging. The nuances of the feelings I so desperately wanted to communicate felt impossible to express. More than anything, I didn't want to intrude. For the past four years Nami and Emo Boo's apartment had served as a revolving door for dying guests. Now that my mother had passed away, the last thing I wanted was to be a reminder of dark times, a burden that Nami felt the need to shoulder.

I often thought of her while going through old letters and photographs among my mother's things, and I struggled to decide whether I should share them with her or shield her from them. The photographs made me feel closer to my mother. The ones she inherited after Eunmi died were still new to me. It was thrilling to see her as a child, with her short hair, wearing sneakers, in sepia, to see the three sisters as children, my grandparents young and attractive.

But I wondered if for Nami it would be different. A candid color photograph taken in some type of banquet hall showed the three sisters lined up oldest to youngest, dancing the conga with their parents. They were dressed up as if for a wedding. Elegant patterned wallpaper and matching drapes hung in the background. My grandfather led the line with a white tie and a fashionable tan suit. Halmoni, dressed in a pink blazer, held on to his waist from behind. Nami was in the center, eyes closed, mid-laugh, holding on to her mother's hips. She faced the camera, unaware of its presence, wearing oversized pearl earrings and a bright turquoise dress. My mother was behind her, her hair in a puffy perm with bangs, looking ever so stylish in a black tuxedo. Eunmi, the caboose, dressed modestly in a dark blue patterned dress with flowers. All of them were facing forward, captured in profile. It was the only photograph I'd ever seen where Halmoni was smiling.

They were all ghosts now. Only the center remained. I tried

to observe the photograph from Nami's vantage, imagining their bodies slowly fading from the frame in a postproduction dissolve, like in the movies where a character goes back in time and changes the circumstances of their present.

My mother once told me about a time when Nami went to see a fortune-teller. She was told she was like a giving tree. Her destiny was to shelter and to nurture, to stand calm and tall and shade whomever lay beneath, but at her base, there would always be a little axe, slowly striking at her trunk, slowly wearing her away.

All I could think of now was, Am I the little axe? Nami deserved space and privacy and a quiet, calm household. I was reluctant to intrude on that, but I also felt like she was the only person left who could understand how I really felt.

IN LATE MARCH, just a few days before my twenty-sixth birthday, my father took Peter and me to the airport. We hugged goodbye, full of mixed emotions. Our departure brought the first chapter of our mourning to a close, and as much as my father and I worried about each other getting on with life, attempting to pick up the pieces, we were equally relieved to be rid of each other.

It was Peter's first time visiting Asia and I was excited for him to experience the pilgrimage I'd grown up making every other year. My mother and I always flew Korean Air to Seoul. She would grab a Korean newspaper, neatly pressed from the stacks set out at the end of the jet bridge, and buckle in, excited to scan the familiar text to which she hardly had any access at home. The flight attendants, all beautiful Korean women with long black hair and perfectly smooth, milky complexions, would take their final turns up and down the aisles and bit by bit, as on the pilgrimage to H Mart, the transient space we moved through acquired contour and color, the impression of our destination engendered long before our final descent as if produced by the pressurized cabin.

We were already in Korea, the familiar lilts and rhythms of its language leaping from neighboring seats, the stewardesses marching with perfect posture in their pressed powder-blue jackets, matching neckerchiefs, khaki skirts, and black high heels. Mom and I would share bibimbap with gochujang that came from miniature travel-toothpaste-sized tubes and we'd hear calls from those still hungry for Shin Cup.

As Peter and I took our seats the first signs of the illusion flashed again, and over the turbine hum the familiar sounds of the Korean language washed over me. Unlike the second languages I attempted to learn in high school, there are Korean words I inherently understand without ever having learned their definition. There is no momentary translation that mediates the transition from one language to another. Parts of Korean just exist somewhere as a part of my psyche—words imbued with their pure meaning, not their English substitutes.

In my formative first year, I must have heard far more Korean than English. While my father was away at work, a house full of women would sing lullabies, putting me to sleep with "jajang jajang" and celebratory coos in Hangul phrases like "Michelle-ah" and "aigo chakhae." The television ran in the background—Korean news, cartoons, and dramas filling the rooms with more language. Over it all, my grandmother's thunderous voice bellowed, punctuating every sustained vowel and singsong rhythm with the distinctly Korean growl that emerged from deep within the throat to exaggerate, like the sound of a hissing cat or someone hawking a loogie.

My first word was Korean: *Umma*. Even as an infant, I felt the importance of my mother. She was the one I saw most, and on the dark edge of emerging consciousness I could already tell that she was mine. In fact, she was both my first and second words: *Umma,* then *Mom.* I called to her in two languages. Even then I must have known that no one would ever love me as much as she would.

The journey that once filled me with such excitement now filled me with fear as I realized that this would be the first time Nami and I would speak without Eunmi or my mother or Seong Young on hand to translate. We'd have to figure out how to communicate without an intermediary.

How could I expect to sustain a relationship with Nami on the vocabulary of a three-year-old? How could I ever sufficiently express the internal conflict I felt? Without my mother, did I have any real claim to Korea or her family? And what was the Korean word for "little axe"?

When I was a kid, my aunts used to tease me, asking if I was a rabbit or a fox.

I would say, "I'm a rabbit! Tokki!"

And then they would say, "Ah nee, Michelle yeou!" No, Michelle is a fox!

No, no, I would insist, I am a rabbit!

And we would go back and forth, until finally they relented. I was smart and good, like a rabbit, not mischievous and conniving.

Did Nami still think of me as the spoiled, sulking little girl her sister brought around every other summer? The one that fussed over the smoke in a fancy barbecue restaurant, complaining it stung her eyes and throat. The one who forced her son to chase her up the apartment stairs while he sweated through his clothes, worrying she'd get lost on her own. After all, it was Nami who coined the term "Famous Bad Girl."

———

"SO TIRED! MUST!" Nami shouted little bits in English. "Good good! Relax!" "You hungry? How about?"

She wore a long, loose housedress. Her hair was cut in a neat bob and dyed dark brown with a hint of auburn. Leon, Eunmi's orphaned toy poodle, ran yipping around our ankles as we exited the elevator and went inside. Nami guided us to the guest room and showed us where to store our luggage. She took Peter out to one of the balconies where she'd placed an ashtray with a wet tissue even though she'd quit smoking more than twenty years ago.

"Smoking here," she said. "No problem!"

She placed a welcoming palm on Peter's back and steered him over to the robotic massage chair in the living room. It looked like a transformer. It was large and high-tech, made of glossy beige plastic with a color-changing LED strip along its side. The seat was smooth brown leather.

"Relax!" she said, pushing the buttons of the remote control. The chair began to recline and the footrest lifted his legs. Sounds like soft little sneezes escaped as it compressed and released air, squeezing his arms and legs while the mechanism beneath the leather pushed and prodded his back and neck.

"Very nice!" Peter exclaimed politely.

Emo Boo returned home from the oriental medicine hospital in a gray suit. He shimmied over quickly to shake Peter's hand.

"Nice to meet you—Peter!" he said. He enunciated firmly, his speech jolting forward into pregnant pauses, like someone toggling rapidly between the accelerator and the brake, as he took time to search for words and prepare pronunciations. "Do you have pain? Where is—the pain? I am—doctor."

He zipped out of sight and Nami spread blankets for us on the floor. Peter and I lifted our shirts and lay down on our stomachs. Having changed into a matching set of blue pajamas with little cartoon foxes, Emo Boo returned and placed suction cups on our backs, squeezing the trigger of what looked like a small plastic gun to remove the air. Deftly and nimbly, he inserted acupuncture needles along our necks and shoulders. After twenty minutes, Nami assisted like a nurse, collecting the cups and needles as he removed them.

Drowsy and jet-lagged, I remained prostrate on the living room floor, drifting in and out of sleep. My eyelids were heavy and I felt my aunt cover me with a light blanket. The anxiety I had carried melted away in her maternal presence. It felt nice to be cared for.

WHEN I WOKE in the morning, Nami was up already preparing breakfast.

"Jal jass-eo?" I said, asking if she slept well. She had her back to me, bent over the stove. She turned, wide-eyed, holding a pair of grease-tipped chopsticks in one hand, and put her free palm over her heart.

"Kkamjjag nollasseo! You sound just like your mom," she said.

Nami prepared a Western breakfast for Peter and a Korean breakfast for me. For Peter, fried eggs and buttered toast with the crust cut off and a salad of halved cherry tomatoes, red cabbage, and iceberg lettuce. For me, she got out Tupperware containers and refried some jeon. I watched over her shoulder as the grease bubbled under the egg-battered pancakes. Oysters, small fish fillets, sausage patties, all battered in flour and egg, fried and dipped in soy sauce. She served them alongside a steaming pot of kimchi jjigae. She opened a plastic single of seaweed and set it near my bowl of rice just like my mother used to.

My birthday arrived four days into our stay. For the occasion, Nami made miyeokguk, a hearty seaweed soup full of nutrients that pregnant women are encouraged to eat postpartum. Traditionally, you eat it on your birthday in celebration of your mother.

It felt sacred now, imbued with new meaning. I drank the broth gratefully, chewing on bits of soft, slick seaweed, the taste conjuring the image of some ancient sea deity washed ashore, feasting naked among the sea foam. It soothed me, as if I were back in the womb, free floating.

I WAS HUNGRY to talk to Nami but words failed me. We communicated as best we could, our conversation interrupted by long pauses as we fumbled through our phones for translations.

"Really, thank you so much, Aunt," I said in Korean one night over beers and cake at her kitchen table. Then I typed into Google Translate: "I don't want to be a burden." I passed her my phone to read it and she shook her head.

"No! No!" she said in English. Then she spoke Korean into her translation app. She held up the phone for me to see. In big letters it read "That's blood ties" with the Korean text above it. "That's blood ties," the robot read out loud. The voice's pacing was all wrong, slow to process the contraction and quick between "blood" and "ties," pronouncing the syllables without regard for one another. There was so much I wanted to say to Nami. I thought of all the years my mother had taken me to Korean school, how I begged her every week to let me skip it and enjoy my Friday night with my friends. All the money and time I wasted. All the times she told me I'd regret treating the lessons as a drag one day.

She was right about everything. Sitting across from Nami, I felt so fucking stupid I wanted to throw my head through a wall.

"Uljima, Michelle," she said as tears started to form and roll down my cheeks. Don't cry.

I wiped my eyes with the base of my palms.

"Umma always said save your tears for when your mother dies," I said with a laugh.

"Halmoni also say this one," she said. "You and your mom very much same."

I was dumbfounded. All my life I'd always thought it was a particularly cruel motto, born of my mother's unique style of parenting, an adage on hand for every tantrum I threw, be it a scraped knee or twisted ankle, a messy breakup or fumbled opportunity, the confrontation with mediocrity, my shortcomings, my failures. When Ryan Walsh smacked me in the eye with a plastic hammer. When an ex moved on before I did. When the band played like shit to rooms filled with no one. Let me feel this, I wanted to scream. Hold me, and let me wallow in it. I thought to myself that if I ever had children, I'd never tell them to save their tears. That anyone who'd been hardened with those words would grow to hate them just as much as I did. And now I discovered my rebellious mother had been scolded with this phrase all along.

"When I was young she told me she threw away a baby," I said in Korean, not knowing the word for *abortion*. "She had so many secrets."

"I know," Nami said in English. "I think . . . Your mom think . . . Come to Korea too hard with two baby."

Nami pantomimed cradling two infants, one on either side. I had never really believed that I was the cause of my mother's abortion when she hurled it at me in anger years ago, but I had also never found an explanation to the contrary. A little girl, occupied by my own blissful excursions, I never realized just how important these trips had been for her, how much this country was a part of her.

I wondered if the 10 percent she kept from the three of us who knew her best—my father, Nami, and me—had all been different, a pattern of deception that together we could reconstruct. I wondered if I could ever know all of her, what other threads she'd left behind to pull.

ON OUR FINAL NIGHT in Seoul, Nami and Emo Boo took us to Samwon Garden, a fancy barbecue spot in Apgujeong, a neighborhood my mom once described as the Beverly Hills of Seoul. We entered through the beautiful courtyard garden, its two man-made waterfalls flowing under rustic stone bridges and feeding the koi pond. Inside the dining room were heavy stone-top tables, each equipped with a hardwood charcoal grill. Nami slipped the waitress twenty thousand won, and our table quickly filled with the most exquisite banchan. Sweet pumpkin salad, gelatinous mung-bean jelly topped with sesame seeds and scallions, steamed egg custard, delicate bowls of nabak kimchi, wilted cabbage and radish in salty, rose-colored water. We finished the meal with naengmyeon, cold noodles you could order bibim, mixed with gochujang, or mul, served in a cold beef broth. I chose the latter.

"Me too! I like mul naengmyeon," Nami said. "Your umma also. This is our family style. He is bibim." She pointed at Emo Boo. When the noodles arrived, she tapped her metal bowl with her spoon. "This is Pyongyang style." She gestured back to Emo Boo's bowl. "This is Hamhung."

Naengmyeon is a North Korean specialty, where the cold climate and mountainous terrain are better suited to furrows of buckwheat and root vegetables than the paddy fields of rice that line the rural river valleys further down the peninsula. Nami was referring to its two largest cities, Pyongyang, North Korea's capital, less than two hundred miles from Seoul, and Hamhung, up the northeastern coast. Both styles of the cold noodle dish became popular in South Korea by way of northerners who fled south during the Korean War, bringing their regional preferences with them. The leaders of the two Koreas, Kim Jong-un and Moon Jae-in, would later share a bowl of mul naengmyeon at the inter-Korean summit. It was the first time a North Korean leader had crossed the thirty-eighth parallel since the end of the war more than sixty years earlier, a historic event that prompted long lines for naengmyeon restaurants across the country, sparking a collective appetite for a dish seen as a promising symbol of peace.

I tried to explain to Nami how much it meant to me to share food with her, to hear these stories. How I'd been trying to reconnect with memories of my mother through food. How Kye had made me feel like I wasn't a real Korean. What I was searching for when I cooked doenjang jjigae and jatjuk on my own, the psychological undoing of what I felt had been my failures as a caretaker, the preservation of a culture that once felt so ingrained in me but now felt threatened. But I couldn't find the right words and the sentences were too long and complicated for any translation app, so I quit halfway through and just reached for her hand and the two of us went on slurping the cold noodles from the tart, icy beef broth.

PETER AND I continued with our honeymoon. We visited Gwangjang Market in one of Seoul's oldest neighborhoods, squeezing past crowds of people threading through its covered alleys, a natural maze spontaneously joined and splintered over a century of accretion. We passed busy ajummas in aprons and rubber kitchen gloves tossing knife-cut noodles in colossal, bubbling pots for kalguksu, grabbing fistfuls of colorful namul from overbrimming bowls for bibimbap, standing over gurgling pools of hot oil, armed with metal spatulas in either hand, flipping the crispy sides of stone-milled soybean pancakes. Metal containers full of jeotgal, salt-fermented seafood banchan, affectionally known as rice thieves, because their intense, salty flavor cries out for starchy, neutral balance; raw, pregnant crabs, floating belly up in soy sauce to show off the unctuous roe protruding out from beneath their shells; millions of minuscule peach-colored krill used for making kimchi or finishing hot soup with rice; and my family's favorite, crimson sacks of pollack roe smothered in gochugaru, myeongnanjeot.

The pungent aroma reminded me of trips with my mother and her sisters to a high-end grocery on the basement floor of a department store in Myeong-dong. An ajumma in a cloth hair wrap and matching apron would call out "Eoseo oseyo" and extend a toothpick skewered with different types of jeotgal to try. The sisters would sample each and discuss, then have the winner wrapped in fifty layers of plastic until it was the size of a football for us to haul home. Sometimes Mom would buy an extra suitcase just to bring it back to Eugene, and every time she served the roe with a side of rice at home, a tiny pool of sesame oil dribbled over the top, I would close my eyes and hear my aunts in careful deliberation.

From Seoul, Peter and I took a train south to Busan, South Korea's second-largest city. A bottle of champagne was set out on the hotel bed with a note that read "Mr and Mrs Michelle, Congratulations on your weeding." It rained all three days we were there but, undeterred, we bathed in the rooftop pools of the luxurious hotel Nami had booked us as a wedding present, the cold rain creating ripples in the water as we looked out at the East Sea.

We visited Jagalchi Fish Market, the rain still beating down on the beach umbrellas and tarp awnings that made up its patchwork roof, dripping down on red plastic basins and bright turquoise colanders filled with the bounty of the sea, spraying piles of cockles and scallops still enclosed in their ribbed shells and long, silvery beltfish hanging limply like neckties over a wooden pallet set out on the wet pavement.

We brought back hwe from the market and set our takeout containers down on the white hotel bedspread. We ate slices of whitefish sashimi, Korean style, freshly killed, still chewy, wrapped in red leaf lettuce and dipped in ssamjang and gochujang with vinegar, washing it down with big bottles of Kloud and shots of Chamisul.

We flew to Jeju Island and hiked to Cheonjiyeon Waterfall, watching the water spume into a clear rocky pool beneath. We walked steep roads along walls of black basalt, eating through a bag of fresh tangerines, then along the beaches, where the water was still too cold to swim. We ate even more fresh seafood: nakji bokkeum, stir-fried octopus; maeuntang, spicy fish stew; and the Jeju specialty, black pig barbecue wrapped in sesame leaves.

Thick strips of samgyupsal sizzled over hot coals, clinging stubbornly to the wire grill as an ajumma came to cut it into bite-sized pieces with a pair of kitchen scissors. I thought of my mother and her butane burner, wearing a blue summer dress with straps that tied over her shoulders, cooking pork belly ssam or grilling steaks and corn on the wooden deck that overlooked the property. When we finished, my father would collect our corn husks and, as was his habit, hurl them joyously over the railing and out onto the lawn as my mother audibly groaned, mourning the month she'd be forced to witness them slowly decompose below. "It's biodegradable!" my father would bellow in defense, scanning the horizon, the firs and pines that rose out of the browning, sunburnt grassy acreage.

These were the places my mother had wanted to visit before she died, the places she'd wanted to take me to before our last trip to Korea was quarantined to a hospital ward. The last memories my mother had wanted to share with me, the source of the things she raised me to love. The tastes she wanted me to remember. The feelings she wanted me to never forget.

# 18

# Maangchi and Me

Whenever Mom had a dream about shit, she would buy a scratch card.

In the morning, on the drive to school, she'd pull wordlessly into the 7-Eleven parking lot and tell me to wait while she kept the car running.

"What are you doing?"

"Don't worry about it," she said, grabbing her purse from the back seat.

"What are you going to buy at the 7-Eleven?"

"I'll tell you later."

Then she'd come back with a handful of scratch cards. We'd drive the last few blocks to school, and she'd scrub off the gummy film with a coin on the dashboard.

"You had a poop dream, didn't you?"

"Umma won ten dollars!" she'd say. "I couldn't tell you because then it doesn't work!"

Dreams about pigs, the president, or shaking hands with a celebrity were all good-luck dreams—but it was shit in particular, especially if you touched it, that was license to gamble.

Every time I had a dream about shit, I couldn't wait to ask my mom to buy me a scratch card. I'd wake up from a dream about accidentally shitting my pants or walking into a public bathroom to find some extraordinarily long, winding shit, and when it was time to drive to school I'd sit quietly in the passenger seat, hardly able to contain myself until we were a block away from the 7-Eleven on Willamette Street.

"Mom, pull over," I'd say. "I'll tell you why later."

SHORTLY AFTER WE RETURNED to the States, I started having recurring dreams about my mother. I'd suffered one such episode before, when I was a paranoid kid, morbidly obsessed with my parents' deaths. My father is driving us across Ferry Street Bridge and to skirt traffic up ahead, he maneuvers the car onto the shoulder, weaving through a gap under construction and aiming to vault off the bridge onto a platform below. Eyes focused on the mark, he leans in close to the steering wheel and accelerates, but we miss the landing by several feet. The car plunges into the rushing current of the Willamette River and I wake up breathing heavily.

Later, when we were teenagers, Nicole told me a story she'd heard from her mother about a woman who suffered from recurring nightmares that all revolved around the same car accident. The dreams were so vivid and traumatic that she sought a therapist to help her overcome them. "What if, after the accident, you try to get somewhere," the therapist suggested. "Maybe if you try to get yourself to a hospital or some kind of safe place, the dream will reach a natural conclusion." So each night the woman began to will herself out of the car and crawl further and further along the side of the highway. But the dream kept coming back. One day the woman really did get into a car accident and was supposedly found dragging herself across the asphalt in an attempt to reach some nebulous location, unable to distinguish reality from her lucid dreaming.

THE DREAMS about my mother had small variations, but ultimately they were always the same. My mother would appear, still alive but incapacitated, left behind someplace we had forgotten her.

In one I'm alone, sitting on a well-manicured lawn on a warm, sunny day. In the distance I can see a dark and ominous glass house. It looks modern, the exterior made up entirely of black glass windows connected by silver steel frames. The building is wide, mansion-like, and sectioned off in squares, like several monochromatic Rubik's Cubes stacked next to and on top of one another. I leave my patch of grass, making my way toward the curious house. I open its heavy door. Inside, it is dark and sparse. I wander around, eventually making my way toward the basement. I run my hand along the side of the wall as I descend the staircase. It is clean and quiet. I find my mother lying in the center of the room. Her eyes are closed and she is resting on some kind of platform that's not quite a table but not a bed either, a kind of low pedestal, like the one where Snow White sleeps off the poisoned apple. When I reach her, my mother opens her eyes and smiles, as if she's been waiting for me to find her. She is frail and bald, still sick but alive. At first I feel guilty—that we gave up on her too soon, that she'd been here the whole time. How had we managed to get so confused? Then I'm flooded with relief.

"We thought you were dead!" I say.

"I've just been here all along," she says back to me.

I lay my head on her chest and she rests her hand on my head. I can smell her and feel her and everything seems so real. Even though I know she is sick and we will have to lose her again, I'm just so happy to discover that she is alive. I tell her to wait for me. I need to run and get Dad! Then, just as I begin to ascend the stairs to find him, I wake up.

In another dream, she arrives at a rooftop dinner party and reveals she's been living in the house next door all along. In another, I am walking around my parents' property. I amble down a hill, skidding on the thick clay toward the man-made pond. In the field below, I discover my mother lying alone in a nightgown surrounded by lush grass and wildflowers. Relief again. How silly we were to think you were gone! How on earth did we manage to make such a monumental error? When you're here you're here you're here!

Always she is bald and chapped and weak and I must carry her to bring her back into the house and show her to my father, but as soon as I bend down to scoop her into my arms, I wake up devastated. I shut my eyes immediately and try to crawl my way back to her. Drift back to sleep and return to the dream, savor just a bit more time in her presence. But I'm stuck wide awake or I fall into another dream entirely.

Was this my mother's way of visiting me? Was she trying to tell me something? I felt foolish indulging in mysticism and so I kept the dreams hidden, privately analyzing their possible meanings. If dreams were hidden wishes, why couldn't I dream of my mother the way I wanted? Why was it that whenever she appeared she was still sick, as if I could not remember her the way she'd been before? I wondered if my memory was stunted, if my dreams were consigned to the epoch of trauma, the image of my mother stuck where we had left off. Had I forgotten her when she was beautiful?

AFTER THE HONEYMOON, Peter and I posted up at his parents' place in Bucks County. During the day we updated our résumés, applied for jobs, and looked at apartments online. I attacked these tasks with abandon. I'd essentially spent the last year as an unpaid nurse and cleaner, and the five years before that failing to make it as a musician. I needed to commit myself to some kind of career as soon as possible.

I applied indiscriminately to what seemed like every available office job in New York City and messaged everyone I knew in search of potential leads. By the end of the first week I was hired as a sales assistant for an advertising company in Williamsburg. They had long-term leases on nearly a hundred walls around Brooklyn and Manhattan, and an in-house art department that hand-painted mural advertisements like they did in the fifties. My job was to assist the two main account reps, helping them sell walls to prospective clients. If we were going after a yoga clothing company, I created maps that pinpointed every Vinyasa studio and organic health food store within a five-block radius. If we were pitching to a skate shoe company, I charted skate parks and concert venues to determine which of our walls in Brooklyn men between eighteen and thirty were most likely to pass by. My salary was forty-five grand a year with benefits. I felt like a millionaire.

We rented a railroad apartment in Greenpoint from an old Polish woman who'd acquired half her husband's real estate in their divorce. The kitchen was small, with little counter space, and the floor was peel-and-stick checkerboard vinyl. There was no sink in the bathroom, just a large farmhouse-style sink in the kitchen that pulled double duty.

For the most part, I felt very well adjusted. Everything was so unfamiliar—a new big city to live in, a real grown-up job. I tried my best not to dwell on what could not be changed and to throw myself into productivity, but every so often I was plagued by flashbacks. Painful loops would flare up, bringing every memory I had hoped to repress inescapably to the forefront of my mind.

Images of my mother's white, milky tongue, the purple bedsores, her heavy head slipping from my hands, her eyes falling open. An internal scream, ricocheting off the walls of my chest cavity, ripping through my body without release.

I tried therapy. Once a week after work I took the L train to Union Square and attempted to explain what I was feeling, though generally I was unable to take my mind off the ticking clock until half an hour in, when time was already up. Then I'd take the train back to Bedford Avenue and walk the half hour back to our apartment. It was hardly therapeutic and seemed just to exhaust me even more. Nothing my therapist said was anything I hadn't psychoanalyzed in myself a million times already anyway. I was paying a hundred-dollar copay per session, and I began to think it would be much more fulfilling to just take myself out for a fifty-dollar lunch twice a week. I canceled the rest of my sessions and committed myself to exploring alternative forms of self-care.

I DECIDED to turn to a familiar friend—Maangchi, the YouTube vlogger who had taught me how to cook doenjang jjigae and jatjuk in my time of need. Each day after work, I prepared a new recipe from her catalog. Sometimes, I followed her step by step, carefully measuring, pausing, and rewinding to get it exactly right. Other times, I picked a dish, refamiliarized myself with the ingredients, and let the video play in the background as my hands and taste buds took over from memory.

Every dish I cooked exhumed a memory. Every scent and taste brought me back for a moment to an unravaged home. Knife-cut noodles in chicken broth took me back to lunch at Myeong-dong Gyoja after an afternoon of shopping, the line so long it filled a flight of stairs, extended out the door, and wrapped around the building. The kalguksu so dense from the rich beef stock and starchy noodles it was nearly gelatinous. My mother ordering more and more refills of their famously garlic-heavy kimchi. My aunt scolding her for blowing her nose in public.

Crispy Korean fried chicken conjured bachelor nights with Eunmi. Licking oil from our fingers as we chewed on the crispy skin, cleansing our palates with draft beer and white radish cubes as she helped me with my Korean homework. Black-bean noodles summoned Halmoni slurping jjajangmyeon takeout, huddled around a low table in the living room with the rest of my Korean family.

I drained an entire bottle of oil into my Dutch oven and deep-fried pork cutlets dredged in flour, egg, and panko for tonkotsu, a Japanese dish my mother used to pack in my lunch boxes. I spent hours squeezing the water from boiled bean sprouts and tofu and spooning filling into soft, thin dumpling skins, pinching the tops closed, each one slightly closer to one of Maangchi's perfectly uniform mandu.

Maangchi peeled the skin off an Asian pear with the giant knife pulled toward her, just like Mom did when she cut Fuji apples for me after school on a little red cutting board, before eating the leftover fruit from the core. Just like Mom, chopsticks in one hand, scissors in the other, cutting galbi and cold naengmyeon noodles with a specifically Korean ambidextrous precision. Skillfully stretching out the meat with her right hand and cutting it into bite-sized pieces with her left, using kitchen scissors like a warrior brandishes a weapon.

SOON ENOUGH I was driving out to Flushing to stock up on salted shrimp, red pepper flakes, and soybean paste. After an hour in traffic, I found five different H Marts to choose from. I discovered the one on Union Street in the height of summer. There was a large outdoor area set up in the parking lot with various plants and heavy brown earthenware jars on display. I recognized the onggi, the traditional vessels for storing kimchi and fermented pastes, though my mother never had one at home. Nami told me in the olden days every family had at least three in their backyard. I picked up a medium jar. It was heavy and I had to hold it with both arms. It felt hardy and ancient. I decided to buy it and try my hand at the ultimate trial and Maangchi's most popular recipe—kimchi.

I opted to make two kinds, chonggak and tongbaechu. A giant head of napa cabbage was only a dollar and practically the size of the onggi. Three chonggak radishes, banded together by blue rubber bands, were seventy-nine cents a bundle. I bought six of them, their green ponytail tops overflowing out of my tote bag. I collected the rest of the ingredients—sweet rice flour, gochugaru, fish sauce, onion, ginger, scallions, fermented salted shrimp, and a huge tub of garlic—and headed home.

I propped my computer up on my kitchen table and hit play. I sliced the cabbage in half. It emitted a charming squeak as the knife cut through the base, waxy and firm. I pulled it apart, "gently and politely," as Maangchi instructed, the leaves separating easily like sheets of crumpled tissue paper. The halved cabbage revealed a beautiful inner ombré. Its core and outer shell shone a pristine white, with light-green leaves yellowing in hue toward the center. The largest bowl I had was a turkey roasting pan Fran had bought me as a wedding present. I filled it with cold water and soaked the halves to clean them. I emptied the pan and sprinkled a quarter cup of salt between the leaves, put the roasting pan with the salted cabbage on my kitchen table, and set a timer for half an hour to turn it.

The only ingredient I was unfamiliar with was the sweet rice flour. I learned I would be turning it into a porridge to use as a binding agent. I combined two tablespoons of flour with two cups of water in a small pot, then added two tablespoons of sugar when the mixture began to bubble and congeal. Mine looked thicker than Maangchi's. It was a milky, gelatinous white not unlike the consistency of semen.

It might have been overly ambitious to take on two types of kimchi, but I figured I might as well use the same marinade for both. Before the timer went off to turn the cabbage, I started cleaning the radishes in the other half of my roasting pan. I raked the bristles of my vegetable scrubber across a dirty white radish, but it wouldn't come clean. I decided to peel the radishes, losing a good centimeter of width on an already small radish in the process but revealing a vibrant white. When the timer went off to turn the cabbage, I flipped the halves to soak on their other side in the briny liquid emerging at the bottom of the pan. The leaves were already beginning to wilt.

I used my blender to mince the onion, garlic, and ginger just as LA Kim had for her galbi marinade, and transferred my radishes into the largest pot I had. I rinsed the other half of the roasting pan and combined the blended aromatics with fish sauce, salted shrimp, red pepper flakes, chopped green onion, and the jizz porridge I'd made earlier that had finally cooled. The mixture was bright red and fragrant, and immediately my mouth began to water. When the last timer went off, I washed all the vegetables thoroughly, grateful for my large, albeit solitary sink.

The apartment was hot and all the windows were open. I was sweating and stripped down to my sports bra, conveniently ensuring I didn't get kimchi on my top. Out of space on the counters, I set all my bowls down on the kitchen floor. With the red paste in the roasting pan between my legs, I set the freshly washed cabbage into the mixture. I painted the paste between the leaves the way Maangchi instructed, inhaling deeply to take in the experience. I used my chin to pause the video, since my hands were coated bright red. I folded the kimchi into a neat little bundle, packed it into the bottom of my onggi, and added the radishes on top.

We didn't have a dishwasher, so I spent the next half hour washing my roasting pan and blender by hand, then mopping the stubborn kimchi-paste smudges from the floor. The whole process took a little over three hours, but the labor was soothing and simpler than I thought it would be.

After two weeks of fermentation, it was perfect. The ideal complement to every meal, and a daily reminder of my competence and hard work. The whole process made me appreciate kimchi so much more. Growing up, if there were a couple of pieces of kimchi left on the plate after a meal, I'd lazily toss them, but now that I'd made it from scratch, I conscientiously returned my uneaten pieces back to my onggi.

I started making kimchi once a month, my new therapy. I reserved an older batch for cooking stews, pancakes, and fried rice, and newer batches for side dishes. When I had made more than enough to eat, I started pawning it off on friends. My kitchen began to fill up with mason jars—each stuffed full of different types of kimchi in various stages of fermentation. On the counter, day four of young radish, still turning sour. In the fridge, daikon in its first stages, sweating out its water content. On the cutting board, a giant head of napa cabbage pulled apart from the bottom, ready for a salt bath. The smell of vegetables fermenting in a fragrant bouquet of fish sauce, garlic, ginger, and gochugaru radiated through my small Greenpoint kitchen, and I would think of how my mother always used to tell me never to fall in love with someone who doesn't like kimchi. They'll always smell it on you, seeping through your pores. Her very own way of saying, "You are what you eat."

# 19

# Kimchi Fridge

In October, a year after my mother died, my father put our house up for sale. He sent me the listing. In the top corner was a photograph of the real estate agents, a man and woman, standing back to back in front of a green screen that had been replaced with a stock image of the Willamette Valley. The photo was the size of a stamp, so their little teeth looked cartoonish, like two solid white lines. The man wore a pink shirt with a red tie, and the woman wore a purple scoop neck, the frame graciously cropped just above her cleavage. These were the people selling my childhood home.

The accompanying photographs were unsettling, so familiar and yet so strange in their new context. The agents had advised my father to hold on to most of the furniture until the house sold, and had restaged our belongings to try to appeal to new buyers.

My bedroom's orange and green walls had been restored to a pristine eggshell. The caption read "bedroom #3." The end table that belonged in the guest room had been moved over to make the room look less empty. On top of it was a small clock and a lone

Beanie Baby that must have dodged conscription to the donation piles.

The pillows on all the beds were still dressed in my mother's cotton cases. The tablecloth under the glass-top kitchen table was the one she had chosen, the table's corner the same that had dented my skull when I was five. My parents' bathtub, where my mother lost her hair, remained, but the full-length mirror where she'd spent so many hours modeling, where she witnessed her bald head for the first time, was gone. The counters were cleared of all her tinted sunscreens and moisturizers, a single, clinical bottle of Dial soap in their place. The bed that she died in was still on display in the master bedroom. The photograph of our backyard, where Peter and I got married, was edited in such high contrast that the lawn was practically neon. "Live here," it invited in some new, anonymous family.

I was ten years old when we moved into that house. I remember in the early days how scandalized I was when confronted by the traces of the family that came before us. In the guest room closet, an unlacquered bookshelf with the names of sports teams engraved into the shelves in blue ballpoint pen. A miniature wooden nun standing by a large tree at the bottom of the property that my mother refused to get rid of even when my friends and I begged her, affirming with all the enthusiasm of youth that it was haunted.

I wondered what the new tenants might find of us. What accidentally got left behind. If the agents would skirt around the fact that my mother died in one of the rooms. If some part of my mother's ghost still lived there. If the new family would feel haunted.

MY FATHER had spent the last few months in Thailand and planned on moving there for good once the house was sold. Because he was out of the country, his friend Jim Bailey arranged to ship some furniture from Eugene to Philadelphia. There were three large items: a queen-sized sleigh bed, an upright Yamaha piano, and my mother's kimchi refrigerator, which we didn't have room for in our apartment and would go to Peter's parents' house in the suburbs for the time being.

Weeks went by before I saw the fridge in person. It was Thanksgiving, the second without my mother. I made sweet potato tempura, which was what my mother always brought to Thanksgiving at Uncle Ron's house. I remember on the drive over holding the heavy serving plate in my lap, stacked high with fried, battered sweet potatoes covered in cling wrap. On the drive home, the plate would be empty, and my mother would boast about how much my American cousins loved her tempura.

I bought tempura flour and a giant tub of canola oil and six Japanese sweet potatoes, dark purple in color and white on the inside, thinner and longer than the sweet potatoes sold at most grocery stores. I washed them clean and cut them into quarter-inch rounds. I combined the flour with ice water and made a thin batter. I dipped each round and fried them in the heated oil, working in batches, careful not to overcrowd them in the sputtering pan. I used chopsticks to pull them out once they'd crisped to a golden hue, and set them on a paper towel to soak up the remaining grease. I crunched into a hot fried potato and licked the oil from my lips. I dabbed at the puffed crumbs of tempura that fell from the edges with my index finger. Somehow my mother's had always come out perfectly crisp all around. Mine seemed unevenly battered, but they were close enough, and it made me happy to maintain our family's little tradition.

In Bucks County, my tempura went mostly untouched and slowly deteriorated into a stack of cold, soggy circles. I tried to put my own spin on it, presenting them in little fry cones I'd constructed out of parchment paper so they might seem more accessible, but Peter's family preferred their own traditions, filling their plates with stuffing and green bean casserole instead. Only Peter and his mother made a show of adding my offering.

"Try it, it's like a sweet potato fry!" Peter encouraged his relatives, much to my horror.

"Are these cookies?" Peter's uncle asked.

AFTER DINNER I went down to the in-law suite to return some roasting pans. In the far corner of the kitchen, looking comically out of place beside knickknacks from Chesapeake sailing vessels and relics of Pennsylvania coal country, was my mother's kimchi fridge. I'd almost forgotten Peter's parents were keeping it down here.

It looked like a normal fridge laid on its side, large and gray, its exterior a smooth plastic. It stood just above the hip, with doors that opened upward, so you could peer into it from the top. In Eugene we kept it by the washing machine, and my mother would have to contort her body around it every time she needed to flip the laundry.

In each compartment there were square brown plastic containers to store different types of kimchi. I inhaled deeply, half hoping to get a whiff of the banchan my mother stored for all those years, half hoping there'd be nothing left to rush pungently through Peter's grandmother's apartment. I could swear I detected the faintest scent of red pepper and onion, though it mostly smelled of clean plastic. I peered inside. The containers were filled with something, but there was no way it could be leftover kimchi. The fridge had been in storage for months and it would have been wildly rank and rotten. I grabbed one of the containers, hoisting it out by the brown handles, surprised by its weight. I set it down on the kitchen table and unclipped the plastic lid from the sides.

In place of the chonggak and tongbaechu, effervescent dong-chimi and earthy, life-giving namul, in the vessel that had housed all the banchan and fermented pastes my mother stored and cherished, were hundreds of old family photographs.

There was no order to them, no set time period or landscape. Pictures of my parents before I was born—my father in front of a snow sculpture, hunched over in the cold, his hands in his pockets. He is thin with a full crop of black hair and a mustache, in blue jeans and a tan down coat. The film is Fujicolor HR and the colors have a magical, nostalgic quality.

Photographs of me as a child, in many of which I am naked—on the back of a red tricycle on the front lawn, perched on a kitchen stool by the island, leaning against the door frame with a case of colored pencils and a xylophone mallet spread out before me on the carpet. Crouched on the grass, my hand plunged into a plastic tub of cheese curls, staring at the camera like a wild dog.

I knew it was my mother behind the lens. Capturing and preserving me. My simple joys. My interior worlds. In one photograph I am lying on a small quilt, unfurled in the living room, bathed in a patch of light coming in from the north-facing window. I remember pretending to float on a body of water, the articles spread out on the patchwork, my sole possessions on my makeshift raft. There is another photo taken from far away, and while the picture shows only a lone toddler in the driveway, seated on a towel one can only guess is a magic carpet drifting on a crosswind, I can also see my mother. I can see her, although she is out of frame, at the top of the stairs, disposable camera pressed against one eye, watching me all along from the doorway. I can hear her instructing me to curtsy in front of a children's rocking chair in the yellow dress she maneuvered me into, instructing "Man seh" as I pulled my head through its collar, my arms through its sleeves, the Mickey Mouse knee-highs she bundled in her hands before wriggling onto my feet.

I search for her in the surroundings, the painted Dutch houses and the porcelain ballerinas and the crystal animal figurines. And I can see it in all my expressions as I regard her—searching for her approval, caught in the act, blissfully occupied by a gift she has given me.

I called for Peter to look, tearing up as I sorted through the pile. I passed the baby photographs around to his grandmother and his mother.

"That's one adorable little Korean," his grandmother said, squinting as she held the photo close to her face.

"And god, that dress," Fran squealed, singling out a photograph in the small stack amassed in her lap. "You can tell your mother just adored dressing you up."

IN THE OLD PLAYROOM, where we spent the night at Peter's parents', I took the photographs out and went through them again while Peter was sleeping. My favorites were the mistakes, ones of my mother that were objectively bad. Her eyes closed, accidentally blinking and unaware. An impromptu photo shoot at the local Rite Aid to finish off the reel. Smiling and posing in front of the cardboard Valentine's Day decor, standing beside a coin-operated kiddie ride, the aisle of wine bottles, the lawn chair display. A surprise shot at the garage door, halfway through closing the trunk of her white Isuzu Trooper. It's like I'm there, watching her edge along the driver's side and come around the car to unload groceries into the house, wearing large sunglasses, as always, her mouth halfway open as if in midsentence, I can hear her call to me to put down the camera.

Candid photos where she's not composed. Where she sits on the couch and I can see her affection radiating toward me, unaware, my back turned as I open a gift from Eunmi. Leaning back in a chair, about to take a sip of beer. Sitting on the living room carpet of our old home, watching something off camera, her nightgown falling off one of her shoulders. I can see the vaccination scar on her upper arm, the one that looked like she'd been burned by a car lighter, how it stoked all her fears that I too would have scars someday. That it was her duty to protect me from everything I might regret.

She was my champion, she was my archive. She had taken the utmost care to preserve the evidence of my existence and growth, capturing me in images, saving all my documents and possessions. She had all knowledge of my being memorized. The time I was born, my unborn cravings, the first book I read. The formation of every characteristic. Every ailment and little victory. She observed me with unparalleled interest, inexhaustible devotion.

Now that she was gone, there was no one left to ask about these things. The knowledge left unrecorded died with her. What remained were documents and my memories, and now it was up to me to make sense of myself, aided by the signs she left behind. How cyclical and bittersweet for a child to retrace the image of their mother. For a subject to turn back to document their archivist.

I had thought fermentation was controlled death. Left alone, a head of cabbage molds and decomposes. It becomes rotten, inedible. But when brined and stored, the course of its decay is altered. Sugars are broken down to produce lactic acid, which protects it from spoiling. Carbon dioxide is released and the brine acidifies. It ages. Its color and texture transmute. Its flavor becomes tarter, more pungent. It exists in time and transforms. So it is not quite controlled death, because it enjoys a new life altogether.

The memories I had stored, I could not let fester. Could not let trauma infiltrate and spread, to spoil and render them useless. They were moments to be tended. The culture we shared was active, effervescent in my gut and in my genes, and I had to seize it, foster it so it did not die in me. So that I could pass it on some-day. The lessons she imparted, the proof of her life lived on in me, in my every move and deed. I was what she left behind. If I could not be with my mother, I would be her.

BEFORE WE HEADED BACK to New York, I drove out to Elkins Park. I wanted to go for a scrub at the Korean bathhouse where I brought my parents and Peter the day after they first met. I put my shoes in a small cubby before stepping into the women's dressing room. I found my locker and disrobed. I tried to take my time and be neat, folding my clothes into a compact pile, my body naturally hunching to cover itself.

When I was a kid there was a jjimjilbang near Halmoni's apart-ment where Korean women of all generations came to soak naked in tubs of different temperatures and communally sweat in steam rooms and saunas. Every year my mother would pay extra for us to get a full body scrub, and after soaking for half an hour, the two of us would lie side by side atop vinyl-covered massage tables while two bathhouse ajummas in underwire bras and sagging underpants would methodically scrub us, equipped with only a bar of soap and a pair of coarse loofa mittens, until we were as pink as newborn mice. The process takes a little less than an hour and culminates when you confront your own filth in the form of a repulsive patch of curled gray threads stuck to the sides of the table. Then the ajumma dumps a giant plastic tub of warm water to rinse it clean, commands that you turn over, and starts in again. By the time you've made the full rotation, you feel as if you've lost two pounds of dead skin.

Inside there were a few older women in the baths with sagging skin, stomachs that hung. I tried politely to avert my eyes, though sometimes I would catch them in my periphery, curious how the body ages, thinking about how I'd never get to see the way my mother would sag or wrinkle.

After I'd soaked for half an hour, an ajumma dressed in a white bra with matching underwear called for me to lie on her vinyl table. She gave me a look, as if she was unsure of how I'd gotten there. She was silent as she scrubbed, speaking every few minutes only to say—

"Turn."

"Side."

"Face down."

I eyed the gray threads peeling off my body and accumulating on the table, curious whether there was more or less detritus than in the cases of her other customers. As I lay on my left side, just before the final rotation, she paused as if she had only just noticed.

"Are you Korean?"

"Ne, Seoul-eseo taeeonasseoyo," I said as quickly and seamlessly as possible. Yes, I was born in Seoul. My mouth was loose and comfortable with the words I knew, and I said them as if trying to impress her, or more realistically, trying to mask my linguistic shortcomings. The Korean soundscape of my infancy and all my years of Hangul Hakkyo had spawned a literate mimic, and the words I knew would fly out of me with the carbon-copied tonality of the women who surrounded me as a baby, but good pronunciation could only get me so far before I became a stumped mute, racking my brain for a basic infinitive.

She looked into my face as if searching for something. I knew what she was looking for. It was the same way kids at school would look at me before they asked me what I was, but from the opposite angle. She was looking for the hint of Koreanness in my face that she couldn't quite put a finger on. Something that resembled her own.

"Uri umma hanguk saram, appa miguk saram," I said. My mom

Korean, my dad American. She closed her eyes and opened her mouth with an "ahhh" and nodded. She stared at me again, taking me in, as if to sift out the Korean parts.

It was ironic that I, who once longed to resemble my white peers and desperately hoped my Koreanness would go unnoticed, was now absolutely terrified that this stranger in the bathhouse could not see it.

"Your mom is Korean and your dad is American," she repeated in Korean. She began speaking quickly and I was no longer able to keep up. I mimicked the Korean mumbles of understanding, wanting so badly to keep up the charade, pretending to understand long enough to catch a glimpse of a word I recognized, but eventually she asked a question I failed to comprehend, and then she too realized that there was nothing left for her to relate to. Nothing more we could share.

"Yeppeuda," she said. Pretty. Small face.

It was the same word I'd heard when I was young, but now it felt different. For the first time it occurred to me that what she sought in my face might be fading. I no longer had someone whole to stand beside, to make sense of me. I feared whatever contour or color it was that signified that precious half was beginning to wash away, as if without my mother, I no longer had a right to those parts of my face.

The ajumma took a large washbasin, heaved it over her chest, and dumped warm water over my body. She washed my hair and massaged my scalp, then wrapped a towel neatly over my head as I had tried and failed to do myself earlier, attempting to emulate the older women in the locker room. She sat me up, pounded my back with the bottom of her fists, and smacked me one last conclusive time. "Jah! Finished!"

I rinsed off on a plastic stool, dried myself with a towel, and returned to the locker room. I changed into the loose spa clothes, an oversized neon T-shirt and billowing pink shorts with an elastic waistband. I moved into a warm jade room that boasted some obscure health benefit.

There was no one inside, just two wooden pillows that looked like miniature pillories missing their top halves. I lay down near one of the walls and rested my neck in the divot. The light was dim with a soft orange hue. I felt relaxed, clean, and new, as if I'd shed my useless layers, as if I'd been baptized. The floor was heated and the temperature of the room was perfectly warm, like the inside of a healthy human body, like a womb. I closed my eyes and tears began to stream down my cheeks, but I did not make a sound.

# 20

# Coffee Hanjan

About a year after Peter and I moved to Brooklyn, the little record I had written in the cottage at the bottom of my parents' property started to receive a surprising amount of attention. Funny enough, I released the album under the moniker Japanese Breakfast, a name I'd come up with years ago, up late one night browsing photographs of neat wooden trays set with perfectly grilled salmon fillets, miso, and white rice. A small label based in Frostburg, Maryland, offered to put it out on vinyl. My mother's image graced the cover, an old photograph of her in her twenties in Seoul, wearing a white blazer and a ruffled shirt, posing with an old friend. I had two of her watercolors printed on the paper centers of the vinyl disc, the songs I'd written in her memory revolving about their poles.

It came out in April and that summer I was offered a five-week tour opening for Mitski across the United States. At the same time, an essay I had written over the course of a few weeks in the evenings after work, titled "Love, Loss, and Kimchi," was selected as

*Glamour* magazine's essay of the year. The prizes included publication in the magazine, a meeting with a literary agent, and five thousand dollars. I had moved to New York to put my creative ambitions aside and focus my energy on climbing the corporate ladder, but all signs seemed to indicate it wasn't quite time to hang up my hat.

I left my job at the advertising company, and the buzz around *Psychopomp* continued to swell, allowing me to pursue music full-time for the first time in my adult life. I put together a band and we drove down I-95 along the East Coast, across the long stretch of I-10 from the marshes of Louisiana through the empty deserts of West Texas and Arizona, up I-5 along the majestic cliffs and mountains of the Pacific shore, and back through the misty valleys of Oregon, where I left flowers on my mother's grave, the headstone corrected and finally reading LOVELY. We played to a full room at the WOW Hall and, later that year, at the legendary Crystal Ballroom, where sixteen-year-old girls beamed at me the same way I had beamed at the musicians I'd idolized. We opened for bigger acts, and then we began to headline ourselves, out for long stretches of the year, crisscrossing the country.

After the shows, I'd sell shirts and copies of the record, oftentimes to other mixed kids and Asian Americans who, like me, struggled to find artists who looked like them, or kids who had lost their parents who would tell me how the songs had helped them in some way, what my story meant to them.

When the band had enough momentum for it to be financially feasible, Peter joined on lead guitar, rounding out the group with Craig on drums and Deven back on the bass. We played Coachella in California. We played Bonnaroo in Tennessee. We traveled to London, Paris, Berlin, and Glasgow. We had a hospitality rider and stayed at Holiday Inns. After a year of shows in North America and three tours through Europe, our booking agent called me with an offer for a two-week tour through Asia. Naturally, we'd finish in Seoul.

I messaged Nami on Kakao to let her know we'd be visiting at the end of December.

We'd kept in touch over the past year, but the language barrier made it difficult to get specific. Most of the time we just wrote "I love you" and "I miss you" accompanied by various emojis and photos of my Korean cooking efforts. I tried to explain that things were going well, that the band was experiencing some success, but I'm not sure she really understood or truly believed me until I informed her that we had a concert in Seoul booked for the second week of December.

A moment later I got a call.

"Hello, Michelle, how are you? This is Esther."

Esther was Emo Boo's daughter from his first marriage. She was five years older than me and had gone to law school at NYU. She was visiting from China, where she now lived with her husband and one-year-old daughter.

"Nami just told me that you're going to play a show here in a few weeks? Is that true?"

"It's true! We are doing a two-week tour all over Asia and our last show is in Seoul. Peter and I are planning on renting an apartment for a few weeks afterward. In Hongdae, maybe."

"Oh, Hongdae is a fun place. Lots of young artists there, like Brooklyn." She paused and I could hear Nami saying something in the background. "We . . . we are just confused. Is there some kind of office?"

"An office?"

"Well . . . I guess we are just wondering, who is it that pays you?"

I laughed. It certainly wasn't the first time I'd been asked to explain it, and after years of pay-to-play DIY touring I often had a hard time believing it myself. "Well, there is a promoter that books the show, and then we get paid by the people who buy tickets."

"Ah . . . I see," she said, though I had a feeling she didn't. "Well, I really wish I could see your concert but I'll be going back to China before then. Nami says her and my dad are very excited."

THE TOUR STARTED in Hong Kong and would take us to Taipei, Bangkok, Beijing, Shanghai, Tokyo, and Osaka before finishing in Seoul. Each night we played for three to five hundred people. The promoters of each show would pick us up from the airport and guide us through their cities, pointing out the landmarks as we headed to the club, translating the input lists to local stage crews. Most important, they'd show us the best things to eat.

It was a stark contrast to what we usually ate on tour in North America, the long drives fueled by gas station snacks and fast-food chains. In Taipei we had oyster omelets and stinky tofu at Shilin Night Market and discovered what is arguably the world's greatest noodle soup, Taiwanese beef noodle, chewy flour noodles served with hefty chunks of stewed shank and a meaty broth so rich it's practically a gravy. In Beijing we trekked a mile in six inches of snow to eat spicy hot pot, dipping thin slivers of lamb, porous wheels of crunchy lotus root, and earthy stems of watercress into bubbling, nuclear broth packed with chiles and Sichuan peppercorns. In Shanghai we devoured towers of bamboo steamers full of soup dumplings, addicted to the taste of the savory broth gushing forth from soft, gelatinous skins. In Japan we slurped decadent tonkotsu ramen, bit cautiously into steaming takoyaki topped with dancing bonito flakes, and got hammered on whisky highballs.

The tour drew to a close. We flew into Incheon and tracked down our guitars at the oversized claim. In the arrivals hall we were greeted by our local liaison, Jon. Jon had arranged our show in Seoul at a club in Hongdae, the same neighborhood where he ran a small record shop called Gimbab Records. It was named after his cat, who was himself named after the Korean rice rolls that my mother had made when it was her turn to feed the Hangul Hakkyo. He was tall and slim, clean-cut, dressed plainly and conservatively in black slacks and a peacoat. He looked more like a salaryman than a promoter and owner of a cool vinyl shop.

Jon took us out for a late dinner, where we met his associate Koki, a sweet Japanese man with a goofball grin who spoke fluent Korean and English. Koki was forthcoming and earnest, the perfect complement to Jon, whom we struggled to get a read on over kimchijeon and many mugs of Kloud clanked in celebration of my return to the homeland.

The next day we loaded in for the show at V Hall, a club capped at a little over four hundred people. Our greenroom was filled with Korean snacks from my childhood, shrimp chips and Chang Gu honey crackers, sweet potato twigs and banana puffs, slices of chamoe melon and even a small box of Korean fried chicken. Jon made sure that Nami and Emo Boo had a spot reserved on the balcony overlooking the stage. The two of them arrived early with flowers. We embraced and took photos together. Nami taught us the latest trend of posing with your index finger and thumb diagonally crossed in the shape of a heart.

When we got onstage, I took a moment to take in the room. Even at the height of my ambitions I had never imagined I'd be able to play a concert in my mother's native country, in the city where I was born. I wished that my mother could see me, could be proud of the woman I'd become and the career I'd built, the realization of something she worried for so long would never happen.

Conscious that the success we experienced revolved around her death, that the songs I sang memorialized her, I wished more than anything and through all contradiction that she could be there.

I took a breath. "Annyeonghaseyo!" I shouted into the mic, and we launched into our set.

I hadn't believed in a god since I was about ten and still envisioned Mr. Rogers when I prayed, but the years that followed my mother's passing were suspiciously charmed. I had been playing in bands since I was sixteen, dreamt of succeeding as an artist practically my whole life, and as an American, I felt entitled to it in spite of my mother's aggrieved forewarnings. I had fought for that dream thanklessly for eight long years, and only after she died did things, as if magically, begin to happen.

If there was a god, it seemed my mother must have had her foot on his neck, demanding good things come my way. That if we had to be ripped apart right at our turning point, just when things were really starting to get good, the least god could do was make a few of her daughter's pipe dreams come true.

She would have been so tickled to have seen the past few years, me dressed up and shot for a fashion magazine, watching the first South Korean director win an Academy Award, YouTube channels with millions of views dedicated to fifteen-step skin-care regimens. And though it felt contrary to my beliefs, I had to believe that she could. And that she was glad I had finally found a place where I belonged.

Before our last song, I thanked my aunt and uncle for coming, looking up at them on the balcony. "Emo, welcome to my hoesa," I said, extending an arm to the crowd. Welcome to my office. The band posed for a picture with our fingers in the heart pose Nami taught us, the sold-out crowd in the background. Dozens of kids left the venue with sleeves of vinyl held under their arms, fanning out into the city streets, my mother's face on the cover, her hand reaching toward the camera like she's just let go of the hand of someone below.

AFTERWARD, Jon and Koki invited us all out to a vinyl bar called Gopchang Jeongol to celebrate. The name translates to *offal stew*, but that was nowhere to be found on the menu. Instead, we ordered a variety of anju. Impeccable golbaengi muchim—sea snails mixed with a red pepper and vinegar sauce served on top of cold somen noodles, tofu with kimchi and dried filefish jerky with peanuts.

The bar was dimly lit with Christmas lights and blue-tinted LEDs that danced around the walls. It had vaulted ceilings and exposed brick that made it feel like some kind of underground loft. In the front was a stage with two turntables and a DJ playing '60s Korean rock, pop, and folk music in front of ten-foot-high shelves filled with records. Seated at wooden tables, our fellow patrons would burst into song at the sound of a familiar track.

Craig and Deven learned the respected drinking customs—never pour your own drink, pour for your elders with both hands—and Jon taught us games like Titanic, in which an empty shot glass is balanced in a cup full of beer and you take turns pouring small amounts of soju in, until it sinks and the loser has to shoot it back. This deadly combination of soju and maekju, the Korean word for *beer*, is called somaek, a common culprit for the Korean hangover.

We drank cold Cass beer from miniature glasses and poured out green bottle after green bottle of soju, sending shots all around and to Jon in particular, trying to lure him out of his shell. Late into the night, we finally made some headway and he began to talk about music.

As Jon got on to the Korean rock scene in the '60s, I listened with rapt attention. My mom never talked much about the music she listened to growing up. In fact, I didn't know much about

Korean music in general, aside from a handful of K-pop bands that were gaining traction in the United States and a girl group called Fin.K.L that Seong Young exposed me to in the late '90s.

When the bar died down, Jon played us a song by Shin Jung-hyeon, a sort of Korean Phil Spector type who produced sugary hooks and psychedelic riffs for girl groups of the era. The song was called "Haennim," written for the singer Kim Jung Mi. It was a sprawling, six-minute folk song that started on finger-picked acoustic guitar and swelled with melancholy strings as it went on. We listened in silence. None of us could understand the lyrics, but it had a sound that was captivating and timeless and we were drunk and somber and moved.

HEADS POUNDING, Peter and I woke the next day to say good-bye to our bandmates and move from our hotel to the apartment where we'd stay for the next few weeks. We would spend some time with my aunt and uncle, and I would do some writing about Korean culture and the food we ate, how it summoned the memories of my mother I wanted to keep closest.

Nami spoiled us the way only she knew how. She knew where to get the best of everything—the freshest seafood, the highest-quality meat, the quickest chicken delivery, the coldest beer on tap, the spiciest soft tofu stew, the top dentist, optometrist, acupuncturist. You name it, she had a guy. It could be dim sum on the top floor of a luxury skyscraper or naengmyeon down a back alley to some damp patio where a squatting ajumma rinsed her noodles over a drain in the cement; she was always quick to slip them a tip beforehand and ensure we got the best product and service.

In Myeong-dong, she took us to my mother's favorite kalguksu restaurant, which served knife-cut noodles in beef broth, fat pork and vegetable steamed dumplings, and piquant, raw kimchi infamous for being exceptionally heavy-handed with the garlic, leaving you with pungent breath that cast a good three-foot radius of odor.

At Gangnam Terminal, an underground shopping center connected to one of Seoul's major subway stations, we browsed the wares together. I was reminded of all the times my mother and I went shopping, the unique form of encouragement she gave me that I so sorely missed when I went shopping alone. I wondered if the shopkeepers thought that Nami was my mother. I wondered if she was thinking the same thing. Each of us was role-playing in a way, soft substitutes for the dead we wanted so desperately to revive. Anything I paused to examine, Nami insisted I let her buy for me. An apron with a flower pattern and red straps, a pair of house slippers with little faces on the toes. She called Peter over to carry the bags.

"Porter!" she said. We broke out in laughter. She'd surprise us occasionally like that, employing the type of words you'd hear on a period-piece miniseries on the BBC. Outdated words like *convoy* or *barbarian* that she'd probably picked up from a required vocabulary list decades ago, pocketed away somewhere in the corners of her mind.

"Nami, have you heard of Shin Jung-hyeon?" Peter asked, collecting our shopping bags.

"Shin Jung-hyeon? How you know Shin Jung-hyeon?" Nami asked in disbelief. Peter explained that Jon had told us about him at Gopchang Jeongol.

"Your mommy and me, we love Pearl Sisters. This one Shin Jung-hyeon! 'Coffee Hanjan'!"

Nami pulled up a YouTube video of the track and played it from her phone. The album cover was bright yellow with the two sisters posing in matching green polka-dotted minidresses. Shin Jung-hyeon recorded it in the late '60s with the sister duo who performed as the Pearl Sisters. It was their favorite song growing up, Nami explained. When they were kids, she and my mother used to perform it at my grandfather's parties. They would wear their own matching outfits and, since they didn't have go-go boots, improvised with their rubber rain galoshes.

ON OUR FINAL DAY in Seoul, Emo Boo drove the four of us to Incheon for dinner by the sea. Nami slipped the ajumma ten thousand won and ordered seafood knife-cut noodles in a savory broth filled with scallops, clams, and mussels. A plate of fresh hwe, light pink and white, uniformly sliced to be eaten with house-made ssamjang, pickled garlic, red leaf lettuce, and sesame leaves. Firm, briny abalone that looked like little sliced mushrooms, served inside their beautiful holographic shells. Live spoon worms, which looked like deflated, wriggling penises.

"This is the stamina food!" Emo Boo said. "Good for man—power!"

"What's this?" Peter asked, game for anything. He was balancing some banchan between his chopsticks, a chunk of boiled potato mixed with corn and mayonnaise.

"It's potato salad," I laughed.

After we finished our bounty, Peter and Emo Boo ducked into a convenience store next door and emerged with firecrackers, which they promptly set off on the beach. Nami and I watched from inside as the wind whipped at their jackets. The past couple of weeks had been brutally cold, even wrapped in the long down coat I'd bought that could have easily passed for a sleeping bag.

Emo Boo and Peter burned through the rest of the fireworks and returned with wet red faces for a final glass of beer before heading home. The sun came down over the Yellow Sea. The gray sky streaked with a vivid strip of yellow orange that thinned and then disappeared.

"I think Halmoni and Eunmi and your mom is very happy," Nami said. She flipped the heart charm on the necklace I gave her so it faced forward. "They are all in heaven together, playing hwatu and drinking soju, happy we are here together."

We took the exit for Mapo-gu, back toward our apartment. Emo Boo began to reminisce about his days as a student at Hongik University, the college nearby. He had wanted to be an architect, but as the eldest son it was his duty to take over his father's practice. The neighborhood had changed a lot since then, its streets now filled with skin-care shops and clothing boutiques, food carts serving fish cakes and tteokbokki, sweet corn dogs and deep-fried shrimp. Street musicians gathered with portable amplifiers, singing to busy walkways filled with young artists, students, and tourists.

On a whim, Emo Boo suggested we end the night with karaoke. He turned the car down an alley over which an illuminated sign read NORAEBANG. Inside, a disco ball rotated, swirling squares of light across the dim purple-hued room.

Nami scrolled through the options on the touchscreen and found "Coffee Hanjan." The song opened with a slow, drawling cymbal, the twang of a noodling guitar fading in over the build. When the lead line finally came in, I could have sworn I'd heard it before. Maybe they sang it together at the noraebangs we went to when I was younger. The lyrics slowly faded onto the screen as the long instrumental intro came to an end. Nami passed me the second wireless microphone. She took my hand and pulled me toward the screen, facing me as she began to sing. I swayed back and forth with her, squinting to try to sound out the vowels and keep up with the melody, a melody I searched for deep within a memory that may or may not have even existed, or a memory that belonged to my mother that I had somehow accessed. I could feel Nami searching for something in me that I had spent the last week searching for in her. Not quite my mother and not quite her sister, we existed in that moment as each other's next best thing.

Peter and Emo Boo clapped in time with tambourines that lit up multicolored LEDs every time they were struck. I tried my best to sing along. I wanted to do all I could to help her resuscitate the memory. I chased after the Korean characters that seemed highlighted at the breakneck speed of a pinball. I let the lyrics fly from my mouth always just a little bit behind, hoping my mother tongue would guide me.

## ACKNOWLEDGMENTS

I must first thank Daniel Torday, a vital mentor who had to read a lot of really, really horrible writing while I was in college and somehow still managed to believe in me after it all. I owe what seems like everything I know about writing to your teaching.

Thank you to Brettne Bloom, the most wonderful agent, champion, and friend. You truly changed my whole life and made it so much fun along the way.

Thank you to my editor Jordan Pavlin, whose gifted counsel and thoughtful support helped see this book to its completion.

Thank you to Robin Desser for giving this story a home at Knopf. Your great wisdom and insight shaped it into a far greater book than I could have crafted on my own.

Thank you to everyone at Knopf who made me feel so welcome in a home with such prestigious residents. I'm humbled by your passion and encouragement.

Thank you to Michael Agger and *The New Yorker* for the tremendous opportunity that jump-started *Crying in H Mart*.

Thank you to Ryan Matteson for your tireless belief in my worth.

Thank you to Maangchi for sharing your wealth of knowledge with the world. You are a light that has guided so many in search of connection and meaning. I'm grateful for your warmth and generosity.

Thank you to Adam Schatz and Noah Yoo for your valuable time and discerning feedback.

Thank you to Nami Emo for opening your arms to me even when it may have been easier on your heart to turn away. It has been a gift to have grown so much closer these past few years, despite its root in our shared grief. It's not lost on me how much you have given, and I will treasure the memories you've shared with me forever. That's blood ties.

Thank you to Emo Boo, Esther, and Seong Young, the last of my Korean family. Thank you to Fran and Joe Bradley, my new family.

And above all, thank you to Peter Bradley, who suffered so many moods over the course of this book, and tempered and tolerated the many bouts of both megalomania and utter despair that came with writing it. What an absolute privilege to have you as a first reader and editor and most perfect companion. How did I get so lucky to have tricked you into marrying me? I love every single thing about you. Thank you most of all.